THE ROAD TO
POSITIVE DISCIPLINE

The Road To Positive Discipline: A PARENT'S GUIDE

BY JAMES C. TALBOT

EDITED BY BRIAN TALBOT

TNT Publishing
Los Angeles, CA

Published by TNT Publishing
Copyright © 2009 by James C. Talbot

All rights reserved under Copyright Conventions.
Published in the United States of America by
TNT Publishing, Los Angeles, CA.

Library of Congress Control Number: 2009901233
ISBN 978-0-578-01058-8

Cover Design by Brian Talbot

*This work is dedicated to
A.S. Neill of Summerhill School fame
and to my son, Brian, who
inspired and edited this book*

CONTENTS

PREFACE

How does a parent understand Positive Discipline without being cognizant of, and responsive to, the problems associated with negative discipline?

Many of us have heard it said that children are our future. It's a statement that may seem nebulous to some, while others might view our future as being determined by a god, Satan, genetics, astrology, or simply by chance. It seems to me that we should place a greater emphasis on the prospect of our future being determined by how we raise our children. For the sake of clarity, the phrase 'children are our future' should rather say, 'we are the future of our children'.

Time and again, we can hear it said that those who fail to become viewed as upstanding or productive members of society have simply avoided taking any responsibility for their actions. Certainly, this type of thinking plays a role when a harsh or abusive childhood makes for a poor defense in criminal trials. Many will posit that they had a hard childhood and turned-out just fine although they possess no frame of reference other than their own. After all, it's not uncommon to hear the absurd statement, 'If I can do it, anybody can'. I'd suggest that some can do it, but others just don't have it in them even when presented with the opportunity to do so. I'll be offering reasons as to why that is.

This book will focus on the premise that we are the sum total of our experiences, and the products of our environment. It's a position derived from a varied number of personal perspectives, related academic studies, experience in the field, being a parent, and long-term observations.

In 1964, after serving 4 years in the Marine Corps, I eventually became the leading Sales Manager for Beneficial Management Corporation. I performed exceptionally well in that position for the next few years. I met my first wife then, although the marriage was short-lived. We separated around the time my first son was born and I played no part in his upbringing. Sadly, I did not see him in person until many years later.

In 1968, as the still ultra-conservative, hard-ass ex-marine, I decided to get a college education on the G.I. Bill. I knew that there was something I was missing, even though I was the company's leading national Sales Manager.

During my first quarter, I read, *Summerhill: A Radical Approach to Child Rearing*, by A.S. Neill. It was an experience that changed my life. It was a metamorphosis of my self-awareness. I found it impossible to deny Neill's logic, his reason, his love of children, and his level of humanity. I applied what he offered in his book to my perspective on life.

I married my second wife and had two wonderful children who we raised together. While in college, I played drums with The Fable, an incredible rock band in the Cleveland area, and graduated from Oberlin College in 1972. My post-graduate studies were conducted at Adelphi University, Case Western Reserve, Bowling Green University, and the University of Northern Colorado, while maintaining a 3.8 G.P.A.

My professional endeavors have included being a social worker, teaching at an alternative high school, youth counselor, group counselor, attempting to found an alternative boarding school, serving as the Executive Director of the Sandusky Valley Board of Drug Abuse, Activity Therapist and Instructor at a private school for the severely developmentally handicapped, college counselor, an expert parenting website author, and childcare consultant. One could say that I've been around the block once or twice.

Why this book? After over twelve years of surfing various parenting websites, and posting/writing as a child advocate, I've come to the conclusion that a vast number of parents simply lack a sound understanding as to why children do what they do. The consequence of this too often results in parents displaying a lack of patience and tolerance in their parenting practices. This is often coupled with a strong orientation toward punishments as a parental teaching method.

It has been these attitudes and perspectives toward child rearing that have served as a major obstacle in my efforts to encourage parents to adopt positive methods of discipline.

In the name of Child Abuse Prevention, I have spent a good deal of time debating the practice of spanking, which is the major factor associated with reported cases of child abuse involving physical injury. If parents can be persuaded to discard this form of punishment, they will find themselves open to alternative forms of discipline. Hence, one will find that I have much to say related to this method of punishment.

I feel it's important to point-out that I enjoyed an advantage over A.S. Neill. Where he took-in troubled older children and developed his philosophy over many years of observation, I was able (with the help of their mother) to employ his child rearing philosophy (self-regulation) from the time my two younger children were born. The result was a wonderful parenting experience. It's often heard said that raising kids is a hard job. I'd love to help change that opinion.

INTRODUCTION

What is 'Positive Discipline'? Well, it's not so much a 'method' of treating children as it is an 'attitude' toward children. It's an attitude that stems from an understanding, awareness, and knowledge related to Child Behavior/Development. More simply put, Positive Discipline reflects little more than the axiom, 'Treat others as you yourself would like to be treated'.

This book will attempt to address the various obstacles standing in the way of parents being able to display the appropriate attitude toward children that is necessary for Positive Discipline to become implemented in the home. I say this because the concept and practice of Positive Discipline is, in of itself, fairly simple as a parenting approach. The key to this form of discipline is dependent on a knowledge and understanding as to why children behave as they do. This knowledge and understanding is the most effective means by which parents can raise the level of their parenting skills, while enhancing the quality of the parent-child relationship.

RELATED CHILD BEHAVIOR

HUMAN UGLINESS BEGETS HUMAN UGLINESS

A theory of human development

It seems to me that if we are raised in human ugliness, we come to identify with it. During our formative years, that ugliness becomes a part of our reality, and we tend to be attracted to that with which we are familiar, can relate to, and identify with. Perhaps we've been subjected to a degree of violent treatment by our parents; often bullied under the guise of discipline; commonly treated with disrespect and rudeness in the home; and shown intolerance toward our inability to learn the rules quickly enough. Compounding this problem is a risk that the same early-on exposure to ugliness might stunt our ability to become that which we might have otherwise one day become. We can be left deprived of our potential humanity and goodness.

It might be said that we are attracted to violence because we have an innate fear of violence and want to learn as much as we can about it in order to avoid it. But, this does not explain why we would actually engage in acts of violence. I would suggest that we engage in actual acts of violence because we can relate to actual acts of violence as a part of our reality; a basic reality established during those formative years. Yet, as a society, we place much more concern on children being exposed to abstract, fantasy forms of violence.

Can it be said that a punitive upbringing leaves us prone to develop an attitude toward others that is punitive/retributive? I believe so. Can it be said that a violent upbringing (physical punishment/spanking) leaves us prone to developing a tolerance for violence against children? Again, I say yes.

I feel that when we have human ugliness forced upon us at an early age, we tend to find ourselves attracted to similar philosophical views, attitudes, and religious beliefs. In the extreme, we might find some who are sociopathic in nature; a member of some neo-Nazi group; a person attracted to the more brutal religious teachings of the Old Testament; or perhaps a terrorist capable of murdering the innocent.

These things are evidenced by the fact that children who are raised having had their emotional needs for love and acceptance adequately nurtured and satisfied simply do not suffer the emotional stunting, the lack of humanity, or the violence-prone behavior that we see in those who have been raised otherwise. On the contrary, what I've seen as a result of such advantageous upbringings are individuals who have been afforded the opportunity to develop their natural propensity toward goodness, altruism, and optimal personal growth.

Standing in testament to the resilience and resolve of the human spirit as it relates to our natural desire to do and be our best, are those who have managed to overcome having been failed as children, yet manage to go on to lead a satisfying, fulfilling life.

DEVELOPMENTAL EMOTIONAL IMPAIRMENT

Perhaps some of us have seen the TV series, *Animal Cops*, on the Animal Planet cable station. Understandably, it may be difficult for many of us to understand the degree of animal cruelty and animal neglect one can witness being presented in these episodes.

I'd like to suggest that the same dysfunctional behavior that sees children killing small animals; that sees people capable of ignoring the needs of their household pets; that finds people with a lack of compassion, empathy, and concern for the well-being of animals, is the same behavior that finds parents treating their children in similar ways. This behavior acts on a continuum of developmental emotional impairment, and is determined by the extent and degree of unhealthy environmental home conditions to which children are exposed.

I would like to submit that authoritarian parental approaches to child rearing (which invariably include the punishment of spanking) serve as a primary causal factor in children failing to have their developmental emotional needs adequately addressed. The consequence is impaired emotional growth and development in children. It might also be suggested that these conditions serve as a causal factor in many children never developing the behavioral state of 'altruism' as an optimal level of emotional growth and development.

ANGER IN CHILDREN

Punishment → Insecurity → Anger

Anger can be a by-product of insecurity if the insecurity (a form of fear) has not reduced the child to the point of succumbing to a state of broken-willed subjugation.

There is also another crucial factor that can be added to the above equation.

Punishment → Low Self-Esteem/Insecurity → Anger

I believe few of us need laboratory proof to agree that low self-esteem and insecurity can be associated with states of anger. We've all observed this association throughout our lives.

Insecurity is a fear associated with self-worth, and fear is highly prone to trigger feelings of anger. We all know the experience of feeling anger, but I'm referring to a generalized angry demeanor, or a proneness to react with anger and resentment.

With children, I believe a general state of anger, resentment, and hostility begins with a failure on the part of parents/caretakers to sufficiently meet their emotional needs. Because we come into this world as social beings, the most primary of these emotional needs in children involves a sense of being loved and accepted.

The adequate satisfaction of these emotional needs cannot be assumed by the parent because whether or not these needs are being met is dependent on the child's perception, not the parent's. If the child perceives that they are unloved, or have lost the love of the parent as a result of being treated in an unloving manner, parents may not be successful in convincing them otherwise; in the present, or perhaps even in the future.

If children feel unloved, they also feel unworthy and inadequate, with no reason to develop a confidence in their capabilities, or in their worth as a person. Feelings of insecurity turn their world into a fearful place to live. They might become hypersensitive to perceived rejection, and other perceived indicators of their unworthiness. These exaggerated perceived threats to the child's well-being, such as parental refusals and restrictions, are highly prone to giving way to anger as a response from the child. Tantrums in these circumstances are an excellent example of this fear reaction being expressed in the form of anger.

The anger stems from fear and frustration, as it does for us all under such circumstances. Like adults, children experience anger when their sense of well-being is threatened. As a result of these circumstances, some children can have their self-esteem diminished to a point where they become broken in will and spirit, at which time they surrender themselves to the 'slave mentality'... the humble servant who nervously bows in subjugation hoping to avoid physical pain, harsh disapproval, or feelings of rejection.

In this regard, it's easy to see how expressions of anger from children should be reacted to with immediate concern and consternation. Parents should not react with more anger and punishment if they feel hurt by expressions of anger coming from their child. Instead, they should immediately communicate their hurt/sorrow rather than letting the emotional hurt transform into anger, which can then lead to a desire for retribution.

Are there appropriate ways to express anger? I don't know if such a thing exists. We either express the anger or we suppress it. We spend a lifetime learning when and how we should express our anger... to no avail. When we express our anger we might hurt others, but when we suppress our anger we hurt ourselves. It's best to avoid the causes of anger to begin with. As I've indicated, the emotional pain that can be caused to the child as the result of negative interaction can trigger feelings of anger. After all, anger tends to do nothing more than to leave us pathetically irrational. This is especially true where children are concerned.

Finally, we should be ever mindful of the fact that a happy child is not an angry child.

DEFIANCE AS ANGER

It should be important for all parents to consider the possibility that children who are viewed as displaying disrespect, willful disobedience, defiance, pushing buttons, or testing limits represent nothing more than expressions of anger and resentment as a result of the way in which the parent has related to them.

One common way in which parents create fear in children is through slaps on the hand, shouts of disapproval, swats, verbal threats, and above all, ritualized spankings. This type of treatment of children instills fear in children, which can then trigger anger. And it's this anger born of emotional hurt and fear that often becomes interpreted as the offense known as defiance.

There is another less obvious, but no less significant cause of angry responses in children. Nothing seems to threaten the well-being of children more severely than behavior on the part of parents that is perceived as rejection. This perception on the part of children generates a fear of losing, or having lost, the love of the parent. For us adults, this same 'loss of love' reaction serves as an explanation for many spousal arguments... raging jealous husbands or angry needy wives are examples of this fear (insecurity). No doubt, adults are known to irrationally behave in a way that acts to push-away the person they want to keep close to them.

It's important to note that children are much more prone to react irrationally to the fear of rejection, or a loss of love, than us adults. The reasons seem understandable. Compared to us, they lack life experience, their perspectives are limited, and they commonly feel a total dependence on parents to meet their emotional needs.

All things considered, it hardly seems reasonable to expect a greater degree of emotional maturity on the part of children than we expect of ourselves or our peers. But, when it comes to children becoming hurt and angry, many of us do expect just that.

A Major Cause Of Tantrums

Childhood tantrums most commonly result from negative interaction initiated by the parent toward the child. I don't think anyone would disagree with that statement. The difficulty that so many parents have in dealing with this behavior stems from a lack of understanding as to how and why this mysterious behavior occurs. What I've discovered as a potentially eye-opening way for some parents to gain a greater understanding and empathy toward this behavior in children involves starting-out by first taking a brief look at our own behavior. I'm still sometimes surprised at the number of parents I encounter who appear to be under the impression that children are born as beings from an unknown species that behave in completely non-human and entirely alien ways.

Having said that, it helps if it can be agreed upon from the outset that adults and children share the same human emotions; the only difference is the level of understanding that comes with maturity. Once that's settled, it then becomes possible to compare children with adults in terms of behavior marked by involuntary, uncontrolled states of emotional distress (tantrums/rages/heartbreak), while keeping in mind that young children are more susceptible to these behaviors due to being subject to high levels of frustration. This frustration can be caused by such stressors as their developmental inability to adequately express their needs, wants, and feelings on a coherently verbal level.

In doing a comparison, let's first look at the most likely reason for adults to lose control of their emotions with regard to a relationship(s). And then, let's go on to look at the factors which are most likely to cause adults to become insecure and prone to emotional outbursts with regard to a relationship(s).

Well, we all know (and have probably experienced) the uncontrollable emotions associated with heartbreak: losing the love of a significant person in our lives, or the perception that we have lost, or are losing, the love of that person. For some of us, the prospect of losing the love of a person who we love and need has been the most frightful, distressful experience of our lives.

We know full well that these situations can turn us into completely irrational emotional wrecks, prone to rages, uncontrolled crying, screaming, and other behaviors that are totally counter-productive to what we really wish. For example, we've probably all witnessed the behavior of jealous spouses who act in a way that only serves to push-away the loved one whose love they are desperately trying to keep. It is a most counter-productive, irrational behavior by any definition.

I illustrate this comparison because for some reason, many parents tend to overlook the fact that children are subject to the same emotional responses and perceptions as adults. As a matter of fact, given the punitive nature of most child rearing approaches in our culture, children are even more prone to suffer the fears of insecurity in the relationship they have with their parents.

Compounding this problem is the fact that young children are as yet incapable of *understanding* the reasons parents refuse them so many of their wishes and desires. Consequently, they are open to fearfully conclude that the parent's love for them may be in question. It might even be the case that a two year old feels that the parent's love for them no longer exists given the limited development of their logic. Unfortunately, we've long forgotten the fear and heartbreak of such moments during those early years... those moments when we became overwhelmed with emotion and lost all control.

Let me see if I can make this point a little more concretely. Let's say you are enjoying a long-awaited movie which is nearing its climatic ending. Your spouse suddenly appears to demand that you leave the theater immediately, but the reason given for this demand makes no sense to you. Might you consider this seemingly unreasonable demand to be hurtful? You might wonder why you are being treated in such a mean and inconsiderate manner. And, if your loved one behaved in such a manner often enough, you might come to question his/her love for you. Insecurity could set-in and cause you to become even more sensitive to being treated in ways that you perceive as being unloving. You might even start to overreact with irrational, emotional outbursts at the slightest hint of 'unloving' behavior toward you.

For some reason, even though young children lack the level of our emotional maturity, parents often assume that their young child knows that they are loved regardless of how the parent interacts with them. A child hearing the words, 'I love you' is meaningless if the professed love is not being felt by the child through demonstrations and expressions of loving behavior.

Some parents even take the view that tantrums are simply a means of 'gaining control', 'manipulation', a way of 'getting attention', or attempts to 'get their own way'. It would seem that these are parents who have apparently never witnessed a child who tried to fake a tantrum. Contrary to popular belief, kids are lousy at faking emotions. Even accomplished veteran actors will say that portraying a complete loss of emotional control is one of the most difficult acting challenges to successfully achieve in a convincing manner.

Some will attribute tantrums to 'bottled-up emotions'. This could be true if the child has developed a fear of openly expressing their emotions because of experiencing previous negative consequences for openly expressing their emotions. This can cause the child to subsequently suppress those emotions. When parents discourage their children from openly expressing certain emotions (most notably anger) the child becomes prone to 'emotional build-up' until that suppressed anger explodes in an uncontrolled tantrum/rage. Consequently, when parents punish a child for expressions of anger, they are exacerbating the problem by increasing the child's susceptibility to tantrums.

Others might point to frustration as a cause of tantrums but, when the parent is the source of the frustration, it is very often the case that the child feels that she/he is being treated in an 'unloving', or 'rejecting' manner. It's a frustration that can build in a child through having wishes and desires repeatedly thwarted or denied in a demanding, strident, or harsh fashion.

Additional commonly mentioned causes for tantrums are over-tiredness, hunger, feeling poorly, or outside stresses. Truth is, when it comes to tantrums resulting from parental interaction, the above mentioned circumstances only serve to make the child more prone to feeling hurt and unloved.

It's important to keep in mind that it is insecure children who are most susceptible to frequent tantrums related to parental interaction. If childhood tantrums are being caused as the result of a parent interacting with their child in a way that may be perceived by the child to be unloving, then punishing the child's tantrum runs a risk of exacerbating the problem.

We can all improve our parenting skills through greater understanding.

TREATING TANTRUMS

How I treat a child in severe emotional distress is the same way I would treat an adult in severe emotional distress. It's a curious thing really when we, as society, look upon emotional pain as somehow less valid or less excruciating than physical pain... especially when it comes to kids. A young child cries in pain over having dropped a rock on her/his foot, and we immediately offer our full sympathy and support. But, when a young child cries in pain over an emotional hurt, so many of us raise an eyebrow, dismiss or ignore the pain, or sometimes even punish the expression of the suffering. I suggest the following (since children are people too, I'll refer to both adults and children as 'persons'):

1. Protect a person who is suffering through extreme emotional distress from hurting themselves, but without using physical restraint unless absolutely necessary.

2. Be there for them... conveying your support, sympathy, and even your own hurt over what they are going through.

3. Stay with them until they are able and ready to talk about what had occurred (depending on age).

4. By all means, make every possible effort to determine the cause of this terribly painful episode, and then make every effort to eliminate the cause. If the person is being exposed to excessive levels of stress/frustration beyond which they are able to successfully cope, attempt to seek ways in which the stressors can be reduced. If *I* have been the cause, I will change my ways as a gesture of common decency.

5. Certainly do not hit or otherwise punish the person. If negative parent interaction served as the trigger, striking the person can exacerbate the problem thereby compounding feelings of being rejected/unloved.

6. And remember, the actual loss of emotional control is involuntary. Kids attempting to fake a tantrum are apparent in their lack of acting skills.

Young persons throwing tantrums are not a given. Although, the high levels of frustration they are subject to experience as a result of their limited developmental skills (communication, gross and fine motor skills), can, on occasion, lead to meltdowns in some cases. The above suggestions are meant to help alleviate the frequency and degree of tantrum behavior.

RESPECT

It's been claimed by many parents that punished children are more respectful than those who are not. I'd like to suggest that this common misperception is a poor excuse for parents to strike or otherwise punish their children.

As many have experienced for themselves, coercive punishments are designed to create fear. The degree of emotional or physical violence inflicted upon children isn't the only influence on the creation of fear in children. Even the threat of violence can cause children to become fearful of their parents. And, it's a fear in children that tends to generalize to other adults outside the home.

The problem here is that too many people equate 'respect' with 'fear'. Those who do should try to get beyond that perception because it's a misnomer. Respect means to hold another in esteem, not fear. To 'respect' means to feel a desire to cooperate and please another who is held in high regard.

Fortunately, parents have a distinct advantage in winning the respect of their children because children are born with an inherent desire to emulate, please, and cooperate. While at the same time holding the parent in such high regard that the parent is the whole world to them. Seldom do we find such opportunities to gain respect with other adults as we do with our own children.

Unfortunately, children don't seem to really learn how to show respect toward others unless they experience being respected themselves. Children must experience respect before they can know what it is, or how to give it back in return.

We need to put behind us all this confusion between respect and fear. Fear equates with nothing other than fear itself, and fear has nothing to do with respect. If one chooses to demand respect, one will produce only the fear of intimidation.

NATURAL BEHAVIOR

The perception that children need to be coerced into a willingness to cooperate with parents remains quite popular.

On the other hand, very few parents have failed to observe that their children tend to copy the modeled behavior of their parents in an effort to learn it for themselves. Can this behavior be associated with willing cooperation? Why not? From birth, few would argue that kids have an insatiable curiosity and desire to learn about the world around them. This curiosity is tied to the basic drive for self-preservation and serves children in their need to develop the skills they will need in order to survive in this new, strange world in which they have found themselves placed. The biological formula seems perfectly logical. The sooner children can master a knowledge of their environment, the greater their chances for survival.

Humanity knows no students who are as eager, as tireless, as determined, or who are as physiologically equipped to process new learning and retain it, than young children. These younger kids not only feel a desire to learn from their parents, they feel driven to learn with an aching sense of curiosity. Given this, when we witness young children going to the extent of actually resisting that which we want to teach them, we might want to give strong consideration to the content and method of our teaching as a probable causal factor of the problem. In doing so, we might come to see that seeking a solution to the 'disobedience' by simply increasing the severity of punishments would have been a most unfortunate, unjust, and unnecessary, course of action.

Some people may feel that this idea alone might represent enough evidence to establish that younger children have a strong propensity to learn from their parents, along with a compatible desire to please and cooperate. But, there is yet an additional, almost equally compelling reason for children to demonstrate these behavioral traits. As a part of what makes us human, we all come into this world with a powerful need for love and acceptance. We are social beings, and these associated emotional needs also create a tendency in children to please and cooperate in order to better serve these needs. No parent could honestly disagree with the fact that young kids have a strong preference for tender love, affection, compatibility, and harmony, over negative interactions, acrimony, or disharmony between themselves and their parents.

While most of us are already aware of this behavior in our children, few of us take the time to account for it. Instead, even in the face of these behavioral traits being in evidence, there seems to be an overriding perception that from the very beginning, children must be forced into cooperation and learning by parents.

Many parents can be heard to say that behavioral/social learning on the part of children must be forced by violent means if necessary, and children will not cooperate unless, from the outset, they are sent the message that they had better obey the parental demands made upon them A sad consequence of these parental notions might be seen soon enough in the form of a self-fulfilling prophecy, when these unloving treatments of young children go on to destroy their eagerness to please, and their willingness to gladly cooperate. This change is especially more pronounced when the forced and unloving punitive treatments of children create in them a level of emotional distance, alienation, or resentment toward their parents.

But, before a time when such circumstances as these could come into existence, we should feel obliged to explore why children would begin to intentionally behave in ways that are contrary to their nature, as well as to their basic emotional needs. There's little doubt many of us assume that because our children have already been told the rules, but nevertheless go ahead and break one of those rules, then they must have done so on a purposeful, willful, and defiant basis.

But, why would toddlers get their hands whacked for touching a no-no, and go right back to it again and again in spite of now knowing better through having been taught more than once to keep away? These are usually the occasions that introduce the concepts of defiance, willful disobedience, and disrespect, into the parenting process. Parents might feel that the child is now 'asking for it', as if this is a child who desires to be treated in a way that countermands the very foundation of their emotional needs, wants, and desires. Obviously, this is not the way in which the human organism normally functions. Instead, the problem is much more likely to represent the child having yet to identify, understand, conceptualize, internalize, or process this learning into their consciousness. We often assume that children have been taught when they haven't as yet learned at all.

WHY WOULD BABY BITE MOM?

Biting behavior on the part of infants reflects just one example of commonly misunderstood behavior.

I think that the most important thing for parents to be armed with in maintaining patience, while holding frustration at bay, comes through an understanding of why it is children behave in the ways that they do. Many parents have found themselves attempting to convey displeasure to their infants/toddlers only to find them laughing back in response. This kind of thing can get very frustrating, especially if the parents are left without a possible explanation as to their apparent lack of ability to convey their feelings to their little offender.

I think kids need, enjoy, and benefit from feeling that they can influence their environment. It gives them a sense of empowerment, control, and a feeling of possessing a certain degree of mastery over their environment, which in turn offers them a greater sense of security. Young children tend to view themselves as helpless and powerless through feeling a total lack of ability to exact some measure of influence over the world around them. This view leaves them prone to feelings of anxiety and fearfulness. It's my theory that this strong tendency in youngsters to seek self-empowerment is tied to our basic drive for self-preservation, or the will-to-live. Children strive mightily to learn about their environment while developing the ability to exert influence in their world. In doing so, they also learn to gain a manageability of their self-determined affairs and activities.

These naturally occurring proclivities serve as a preparation for the time when children reach an age when they will be required to determine their own destiny as an independent, self-reliant citizen of the world.

So, let's assume for a moment that these developmental tendencies provide an indication that children possess an inherent tendency to equip themselves with the survival skills necessary to function independently at some point in their lives. We know that healthy emotional growth and development on the part of children includes a desire for self-determination and independence. This theory offers an explanation as to why these tendencies exist. It would seem to be a reasonable developmental trait for us to prepare ourselves for a time when total reliance and complete dependence on our parents reaches an end. It seems to me that these specific traits, as a part of our drive for self-preservation, can be seen as plausible on a genetically determined basis. I'm not saying we're born as hungry power-mongers with an inherent propensity toward gaining control over others, but I do think we have a need to feel in control of our own lives as a built in survival mechanism. This theory could serve to explain the insatiable curiosity, the desire for independence, and the distinct pleasure kids experience through finding that they are capable of having an influence on their environment through instigating cause and effect (I can still see my son at about age three, doubled-over in laughter at having caused me to fall down dead after shooting me with his 'waser' gun).

All of this then leaves us with a responsibility to teach our kids what particular parts of their environment have been deemed acceptable for them to influence or control according to the norms of society (the socialization process).

Related to this topic is the problem of biting on the part of infants, and my thoughts on this topic serve as a good example of my above comments. In addition, one can see the workings of Positive Discipline.

This infant behavior might be called, 'I want to bite you, mommy'. The effect biting infants are attempting to produce might involve gaining a sense of control and influence in their helpless world. So, perhaps they bite for effect, and initially like the high degree of impact they can achieve as a result of this behavior (unless, of course, the reason for this is sore gums). The problem is when they bite as a result of experiencing an excessive amount of frustration or negative interaction. Well, certainly they are going to eventually learn that biting is a no-no, but naturally, parents want to move this learning process along as quickly as possible.

So, how does one teach babies to bite discriminately (as in teethers) while inflicting a minimal amount of emotional pain upon them in the process? This is a question that explores fairly new territory in the annals of child rearing because just 50 years ago, the question would not have been asked, or for that matter, even pondered in parenting circles. Back then, inflicting some physical pain as a learning tool was the common remedy for teaching any behaviors deemed unacceptable by parents. A likely question back then might have centered on the effectiveness of various methods of inflicting punitive pain that might be used in teaching the child to listen without hesitation.

To begin with, parents might over-dramatically respond in pain and displeasure at having been bitten by baby. The thought process of baby might sound something like this: 'It sure feels good to bite, and I sure made something happen when I did it. I'll just have to learn whether it was a good thing or not, considering all those unpleasant sounds and unsettling faces mommy was making... I do not like that, but let's see what else I can chomp into before I try some food spitting and dish throwing to see things that I can make fly all on my own!'. Another teaching technique parents might want to consider consists of distractedly putting baby down so that mom can better explore her supposed injuries... baby won't be laughing if she/he still wants to be held at the time.

The unpleasant consequences that parents can stage as a drama serve to create the impetus for babies to begin associating the biting of others with unpleasantness. They don't need to suffer beyond very short-lived mild confusion and discontent in order to learn this lesson. Parents can pick their little biters right back up if they request it. The significant learning has already taken place upon their expression of displeasure. Plus, with more negative emotion being directed at the apparent injury than toward them, the likelihood of them feeling that the parent has withdrawn their love from them will be diminished. After all, at this point in time, there is no way for babies to yet understand a reason for anger to be directed at them, and an angry voice aimed at them would accomplish nothing more than to leave them feeling hurt, diminished, and scared.

WHY KIDS LIE AND DECEIVE

While spanking understandably creates the greatest degree of fear in children with regard to the admission of wrongdoing, logic tells us that the same holds true for all punitive methods of discipline.

A 'fear of the truth' can be created in a young child by the parent merely displaying an accusatory demeanor as they interrogate the child about whether or not they committed any wrongdoing. The parent discovers the mess, the spill, or the breakage, becomes emotionally upset, and rushes the child to the scene of the crime. Then, in a menacing, intimidating voice exclaims, 'Did you do this? Well, did you?' The child under these kinds of circumstances might find denial to be more a case of reactive self-preservation than intentional deception.

There is only one reason that kids lie under such circumstances, and that reason is fear, Whether it's the abject fear of physical punishment or the fear of a time-out banishment (or other forms of punishment), the ultimate fear lies in the prospect of losing the love and acceptance of the parent. To young children, those rejecting, hateful, and unloving punitive treatments of them by parents is forever, until such time as they are made to feel otherwise. Young children employ a very fundamental and simple form of undeveloped logic, 'If you act like you hate me, then you must hate me'. Unfortunately, as adults we've long since forgotten the needless high level of fearfulness that this form of logic can generate.

This is a good question for all parents to ask themselves: 'Why do any of us lie about having been the cause of accidents, mistakes, or wrongdoings?' The answer is that we lie because we fear the consequences of telling the truth. It's because we live in a punitive society and we should not be surprised to find ourselves as a society of liars when it comes to admitting guilt.

It's generally a lesson our children learn at an early age; there are times when the truth is best avoided. After all, we humans have a strong tendency to protect and preserve our sense of well-being. And, after all, whose sense of well-being is more frequently threatened and jeopardized than that of a young child?

Especially in cases where children are spanked for expressing the truth, we should expect no less than turning them into little liars who become quickly adept in the art of deceit and deception.

INSECURITY

It should come as no surprise that abused wives will commonly report that being hit by their husband caused them to develop a fear that their husband no longer loved them. That's insecurity. We all know that the jealous husband possesses a fear that his wife may not love him enough to remain faithful. That's more insecurity. It's a fear that is invariably associated with an insufficient level of self-esteem. After all, do we not base a substantial portion of our 'worth' in this world on the amount of love we experience in life?

Anyone who has experienced the fear of insecurity can testify to its debilitating consequences... both physically and emotionally. Where children are concerned, they simply cannot afford to live in an insecure environment. Children cannot be expected to experience a healthy process of emotional growth and development in the midst of an amount of parental negative interaction sufficient to cause them to question the love of the parent. Do we know of a greater fear than the loss of love? Is there a more plausible reason for tantrums than experiencing a fear of having lost the love of someone dear to us, for children as well as adults?

While the spanking of children unquestionably represents to them the ultimate act of rejection and loss of love, other negative interactions with children can also play a role in the development of insecurity; threats, scowls, criticisms, yelling, indifference, banishment (time-outs, forced bedtime), and ignoring or dismissing the efforts of children to communicate. Chronic insecurity in children is no small matter as it can serve as the basis for the development of emotional disorders, behavior problems, and dysfunctional parent-child relationships.

In light of the fact that most relationships involve some degree of negative interaction, it might be suggested that the most prudent way to avoid the development of insecurity in children is to minimize the frequency and degree of negative interaction that is initiated by the parent. At the same time, we *all* tend to thrive and feel secure in an environment of warmth, affection, praise, encouragement, and other expressions of love and acceptance.

Negative interaction with a child too often represents nothing more than a demonstration of our own failings, and it's a high price we sometimes pay when our failings result in failing our children.

THE EMOTIONAL NEEDS OF CHILDREN

It's my strong belief that the major cause of behavior problems in children stems from a failure on the part of parents/caretakers to adequately meet their emotional needs. Following is a list of crucial emotional needs that need to be met in order for children to develop in a healthy manner:

1. Love. Children will fail to thrive in the absence of love, and the development of self-esteem in a child is wholly dependent on the child feeling a sense of being loved and cared for. This is why negative interaction toward a young child carries such risk. It's sad that the definition of this word has become so abused, and convoluted where children are concerned. Perhaps we should start using the word 'adore' in place of 'love'.

2. Security. A child who comes to question parental love is a child at risk for a myriad of emotional problems, along with a much higher probability of developing dysfunctional relationships with not only parents, but others as well. Not nearly enough attention is paid to the fear and misery suffered by an insecure child.

3. Affection. We're still learning about the significance of affection on a child's development. But, as things stand now, I would say that the most important function of affection comes through the crucial role it plays in conveying love, warmth, and acceptance.

4. A stimulating, vibrant environment. This is a fairly new higher need whose significance has been recently established through brain research. There is evidence to indicate that intellectual stimulation during infancy is a crucial factor with regard to normal, healthy brain development, and the creation of new brain cells (which could have a direct bearing on the establishment of intellectual potential).

5. Praise and Encouragement. With regard to the healthy developmental emotional growth of a child, this process is greatly enhanced through children coming to feel that their parents are 'on their side'. Positive interaction with a child serves to enhance their sense of well-being (as it does for us all). If a

child gains a sense of being a worthwhile part of this world through love and acceptance, praise and encouragement, the child is provided with the confidence to actively take part in what the world has to offer.

THE DEVELOPMENT OF ALTRUISM

What will be our saving grace?

The way in which we raise children will determine whether or not our civilization will survive in the long run. Altruism is the key. Altruism is a developmental process that is dependent on environmental child rearing conditions during our formative years.

The development of altruism allows us to become persons who are sincerely concerned about others, as well as the world in which we live. Unfortunately, given the continued propensity for authoritarian child rearing practices in our culture, many children are deprived of the opportunity to develop altruistic tendencies as a developmental stage of emotional growth.

The guilt for this failure of the development of altruistic behavior coming to pass lies in the prevalence of authoritarian parenting practices within our culture. Again, our natural propensity to develop altruism is too commonly thwarted by the oppressive, authoritarian way in which so many children are raised.

We stunt the emotional growth of children by striking them; diminishing them, and making them feel that they have a lesser value in this world than us adults. As a result, we produce adults who are only capable of a concern for their own personal needs and wants... adults who are deficient in empathic behavior. These are adults who lack the ability to look beyond their own short-sighted personal concerns; who fail to consider the needs and wants of those around them; and who lack a concern toward the future well-being of the environment in which we live.

We need to forgo the antiquated, traditional methods of raising children in an authoritarian manner, and turn to the safer, more effective approach to parenting consisting of positive methods of discipline. It's been my experience (including my own parenting experience) that these positive methods have shown themselves to be much more conducive to the development of altruistic behavior in our children.

PARENTING ISSUES

AGEISM

Ageism is an irrational group prejudice based on age. It is just as difficult a social issue to tackle as racism or sexism because these behaviors represent identical characteristics and dynamics. As such, these behaviors are equally difficult to overcome.

The male chauvinist (sexist) views his wife as a sexually objectified possession who is also seen through an attitude that dictates that the wife be held in lower regard than his male peers. As a result of this prejudicial, discriminatory attitude toward the female gender, wives are subject to be treated with what is seen as a justified, deserving lower standard of respect and consideration. This lower standard of treatment is closely associated with women being designated a lower social status than men as a result of their being perceived as the inferior 'weaker sex'. The 'real man' reserves his friendships for other equally deserving men. He 'rules his roost' with an ever present air of aloof superiority over an understandably diminished and bowed 'little lady', who dutifully meets his demands and satisfies his needs in her role as a bought and paid for possession; a possession to be used as a bed-partner, mother, and housemaid. The basis of the problem stems from men possessing an attitude of superiority over women.

We are all pretty familiar with the specter of racism. The behavioral dynamics are the same as those comprising the prejudices of ageism and sexism... the targeted group that's regarded as being inferior is held to a lower standard of social-status, while justification is offered to establish an acceptably lower standard of treatment for the targeted population deemed to be inferior. I should add here that throughout history, the rationalizations used as excuses for physical discipline have been basically the same for women, children, prisoners, and enslaved African-Americans. Typically, these excuses have included striking the offender for 'safety', 'disobedience', or 'defiance'.

In the same vein, ageism involves a perception of children as inferior forms of humanity, and as such, they are regarded as being justifiably held to a lower standard of treatment with less respectful considerations. Children are essentially devalued in human terms and forced to function in the role of 'second class citizens'.

All of these above mentioned prejudice-afflicted individuals present a formidable challenge in terms of effectively instilling either a raised understanding, a higher level of consciousness, or increased levels of empathy through an educational process. To begin with, these are seldom individuals who feel a burning desire to change their existing attitudes toward those they regard as seriously flawed, inferior beings. Secondly, these prejudices commonly represent deep-seated orientations that were instilled in these individuals during their early formative years, which is a time when learned behavior is subject to manifest itself as deeply ingrained beliefs or 'fixed' behaviors.

DISCIPLINE

The concept of discipline does not necessarily involve punitive measures. While discipline is usually associated with punishment, a 'well disciplined' child is not necessarily a punished child. Actually, the root word of 'discipline' is 'disciple', which refers to a student-teacher relationship. In years past, it was assumed that punishment as a part of discipline was a good method of teaching and subsequently this concept eventually became a norm of parenting.

Educators have long since discovered that fear (as a product of punishment) is an inferior teaching tool and can even have a counterproductive effect on the learning process. This is why educators advise against punishments for children who make mistakes while learning their ABC's. We need to take into account the fact that cognitive learning involves the same process for learning acceptable behavior as it does for learning academics. We see parents who want to teach their kids a lesson, but too often find that the supposed lesson is more for the sake of the parent than it is for the kids. Another problem with punishment as a form of negative discipline is that it often does a much better job of diminishing the quality of the parent-child relationship than it serves as an effective teaching method.

Let me say again that the learning process for children is not any different for learning acceptable behavior than it is for learning how to read. While most parents have come to realize that a child making repeated mistakes while learning to read should not be punished for such a failure to comply, some of these same parents persist in imposing punishments for a failure to comply when it comes to unacceptable behavior. It can only be assumed that there is some irrational element of retribution involved on the part of the parent under these circumstances.

It would seem that some parents assume that when it comes to behavior, children should be capable of learning what is expected of them in one short lesson. After being told/warned/threatened of the behavioral mistake, any future repeated mistakes on the part of the child are considered affronts to the parent, with punishment as retribution being a common result.

Through feelings of hurt and rejection on the part of the child, the child may begin to react with anger and resentment to being treated in such a manner... the tragic consequences can be the development of a confrontational relationship between the parent and the child. In this situation, we have a parent feeling disrespected, while the child is feeling hurt, rejected, and angry. This can sadly result in a disharmonious parent-child relationship.

Positive Discipline, on the other hand, involves a patient, gentle, guiding hand that better serves to foster actual learning rather than resentment. Young children are naturally inclined to cooperate and please the parent. But when they are coerced into bending to the will of the parent, they are prone to feel hurt, rejected, and/or diminished. This emotional pain caused by the parent often triggers feelings of anger, resentment, and even contempt. These emotions on the part of the child are too often regarded by parents as good reason for increasing the severity of punishments... thereby setting the stage for the development of a vicious cycle of escalating acrimony between parent and child.

Demands

Unfortunately, there is a commonly found parental attitude toward young children that can serve to set a disharmonious tone for the parent/child relationship from the very beginning.

It's an attitude which assumes that where children are concerned, learning experiences must come in the form of demands, which inherently involve negative parent-child interactions. This double standard to which we often hold children is surely a strange, and even counterproductive, way to establish a productive, fulfilling, and gratifying high-quality relationship.

In a newly forming relationship with another person, we normally establish the parameters of what behaviors we expect by requesting that our wishes be met in a respectful, patient manner (rather than rudely demanding them)... otherwise the relationship may falter. Why so many parents make the mistake of assuming that this obvious principle of human interaction applies differently to children is beyond my comprehension.

We know that young children are exceptional learners with minds like sponges, insatiable curiosity, and an unrelenting desire for increased knowledge. Moreover, they are highly motivated students with unquestioning trust, who are highly inclined to please the teacher/ parent. When you add to this mix the fact that children also possess a strong natural desire to emulate the behavior of the parent, there can be no denying that young children are the best students in the world. It's a fact largely ignored.

Given the above, one of the most effective ways parents teach their children is through 'modeling'. In other words, children will tend to copy or mimic the behavior of the parent. When it comes to expectations, we should allow children to learn at their own individual rate, and stand by patiently until they develop a firm grasp of the lessons being taught. We need to have faith that they *will* learn in their own time. It is counter-productive for us to lose patience and become anxious, then demanding, then punitive.

This modeling form of teaching is especially beneficial with regard to those behaviors we expect of children at a time before they are able to understand the reason for them. The developmentally limited ability for young children to reason soundly is perhaps why they are naturally inclined to emulate the behavior of the parent(s). This is an area of learning where parental modeling can teach children in the absence of understanding. If a parent uses the word 'please', the child will use the word please (according to the level of their language skill development). If a parent displays kindness, the child will display kindness (even before the child is capable of having developed empathy)... this is the value of modeling and how it serves as an invaluable teaching tool.

For example, if a parent wants to make the teaching of bathroom behavior a simple and easy process, they need only adopt an open-door bathroom policy at an early age. That little 9-month-old crawling up to the bathroom door to see mommy or daddy using the facilities is learning a lesson for sometime in the near future. Or, the child might accompany the parent in the bathroom. If silly modesty prevails, the parent should teach these things in an up-beat, patient manner when the time comes. My kids wanted to brush their teeth because I had made a display of having a good time brushing my own teeth while they were still crawling around on the floor.

This leads me to the crux of why so many parents find it difficult to teach their children. A parental proclivity toward making demands often acts to cause young children to develop negative associations with the behaviors that the parent is harshly insisting upon. For example, if brushing the teeth becomes associated with negative interaction with the parent, the child will become subject to developing an aversion to brushing their teeth. I hope this makes sense, because this behavioral phenomenon is a basic cause of much frustration, acrimony, and family disharmony... sometimes to the point of dysfunction. Children can come to forget brushing their teeth, just like we adults forget those dentist appointments as a result of our own aversion to pain (physical or emotional). Why should a child want to clean their room if the act itself is associated with past emotional hurt and pain at the hands of a demanding parent?

There can be little doubt that parents would discover an improvement in the quality of the relationship they have with their children by beginning to seek their cooperation, rather than demanding their obedience.

I think it's fair to assume that many parents are under the impression that cooperation from children must be demanded through intimidation rather than sought through respectful request. These happen to be parents who are under the impression that the development of contention, resentment, and willful disobedience should be viewed as an inevitable part of the parent-child relationship. It's a view holding that commonly occurring disharmony and acrimony between parents and children is simply a natural and unavoidable part of the normal scheme of things.

A good question to ask regarding this issue is why it is that kids disobey in the first place? It does seem inconsistent with how young children are generally prone to behave, doesn't it? Every parent knows that young children generally display a strong tendency to emulate parents and 'be just like mommy or daddy'; and all parents know that kids have a powerful need for love and approval, and seek nothing more than acceptance, affection, warmth, and gentle caring.

These tendencies in children aren't dependent on genetic differences; they are rather very basic, inherent tendencies, which act in direct association with our basic drive for survival, self-preservation, or what is sometimes referred to as the 'will-to-live'. In association, young children need to feel safe, protected, and comfortable. Given these needs, it makes complete sense to say that negative parent-child interactions should be held to a minimum. As social beings, this is a universal inherent human trait shared by all of us as a basis for survival.

When discussing the issue of disobedience vs. cooperation, I think it's also important to give thoughtful consideration to children's powerful need for love and acceptance. With this in mind, it seems reasonable to then ponder the question of why children would appear to deliberately disobey the person for whom they are entirely dependent for their very survival. Wouldn't it follow that, in light of their needs, children would be much more prone to cooperate with the parent as a necessary part of learning the skills needed to insure survival? Especially when taking into account the fact that, in the normal scheme of things, a child's failure to cooperate with a parent is contrary to the function of this basic drive for self-preservation? It should reasonable to conclude that when children lose their normal desire to cooperate with the parent, then the presence of a disruptive factor is acting to impede the development or continuance of this normal tendency.

To pursue this issue even further, the next question that should be considered involves the specific factors in the parent-child relationship that could potentially act to interfere with the normal state of children striving to satisfy their need for love and acceptance. It makes sense to associate this need for love and acceptance with a natural preference for cooperation over disharmony on the part of children toward their parents.

So, why do children defy their parents? Let's clarify and explore the possibilities.

1. There can be no denying the fact that we are born as social be-ings. To even a greater extent than adults, infants/young chil-dren are dependent upon feeling accepted by others (parents) and are extremely sensitive to feelings of rejection or neglect. As with all of us, these feelings threaten our sense of well-being, and we become fearful. If we aren't totally numbed by fear, we tend to react in anger toward those who would hurt our feelings, reject us, or cause us to feel unaccepted and un-wanted. You might be asking how this relates to the issue of 'deliberate disobedience'. Well, I believe the problems start with young children who have not yet reached an age where they are capable of understanding, or conceptualizing, the rea-soning behind many of the lessons we try to teach them.

    We all know that the things that don't make any sense to us are the most difficult to learn. We will usually make a re-quest for additional patience and understanding when at-tempting to learn these kinds of things. It's unfortunate that we so often fail to extend this courtesy to young children. The teaching of manners is one good example of the difficulty kids have with what they can only regard as nonsensical learning... 'Say please, son'. 'Huh?' 'I said, say please'. 'What does that mean, mommy?' 'Just say it'. 'Why, mommy? All I want is a glass of water!' 'You don't get the water until you say, please' 'Mommy, why are you being so mean?' 'Do you want the water or not?'

    This type of scenario often introduces the problem of how we human beings normally react when someone loses patience with us for repeatedly failing to grasp what the frustrated teacher is attempting to get through to us. Isn't it true that we begin to feel hurt and anger as the result of someone losing patience with us? And isn't it also true that we might be prone to express that hurt and anger as a result? Is there any reason to believe that children should react to feeling hurt in a more mature manner than us adults? Much to the dismay of many a child, these same circumstances are interpreted by parents as 'defiance', 'disrespect' or 'deliberate disobedience'. As a result of this misunderstanding on the part of the now displeased parent, the child's hurt and anger might only deepen.

2. If children develop a sense of being worthwhile in this world, they will also develop a confidence in their ability to function independently while, at the same time, pursuing their desire for self-determination as a part of developing a strong sense of self. These circumstances lend themselves to the development of feelings of competence, self-discipline, self-sufficiency, self-assuredness, and a resultant strength that will serve them well when later taking on the various challenges life will place before them. While young children are certainly not yet capable of functioning on these levels they nevertheless possess the desire to function independently. This is a behavior that is indicative of healthy levels of self-esteem, and is something that all parents should desire to observe in their children.

    But, once again, this is another area of child behavior that many parents perceive as a defiant challenge to their authority. Fact is, it's a reflection of healthy growth and development when kids feel the confidence to demonstrate a strong desire for independence and self-determination. Parents should be gently guiding this behavior rather than punishing it as disobedience. And again, to make matters worse, the children have absolutely no understanding of why parents would thwart their attempts to find their own way in the world. The children can only regard being punished for attempting to establish their own self-determined identity as behavior toward them that is mean-spirited, rejecting, and hurtful.

3. Children tend to become generally alienated and angry toward their parents through repeated confrontations, coercion, violence, or other forms of negative interaction. This can result in children becoming contentious, disagreeable, and disobedient. The parent's continued punishments for these expressions of

anger only serve to exacerbate the problem, and a vicious cycle of contention and disharmony can ensue. The probability of maintaining a high quality relationship between the parent and the child is greatly decreased under these circumstances.

4. Children made to feel insecure regarding the love of a parent through excessive negative interaction will sometimes intentionally break rules to test the love of the parent. In extreme cases, some children's self-esteem suffers to a point where they come to feel that they deserve to be punished, humiliated, and berated for any and all infractions, however minor. A child not feeling love is a child who does not feel worth. This is a child who may come to feel not only undeserving of love, but also deserving of punishment.

5. Children who perceive that they have failed to gain the affections of parents through acceptable behavior will sometimes resort to unacceptable behavior in a desperate attempt to gain some measure of attentiveness from parents. In such cases, it might be said that indifference acts as the opposite of love, even more so than hateful behavior toward the child. This idea, as it relates to adults, has been explored by such social theorists as Eric Fromm and Elie Wiesel. Kids don't look for attention by misbehaving unless they have reached a point of considering negative interaction to be more desirable than no interaction at all.

Because of the many demands we make upon young children which are often interpreted by them as mean, unfair, and hurtful, I worry about children who become totally obedient, submissive, and compliant... the state of resigned subjugation. Or, if you will, the authority-directed slave mentality. What concerns me most about the prevalence of authoritarian parenting is that it can serve to break the spirit of children and rob them of an opportunity to develop a level of self-esteem that will allow them to adequately function in the world on the strength of their own resolve.

This authoritarian approach serves to discourage healthy levels of self-esteem, and it should be clearly noted that low self-esteem is associated with all manner of maladaptive behaviors, including emotional disorders, mental illness, violence-prone behavior, the addictive personality, anti-social behavior, and lesser maladies which also act to diminish the quality of ones life. To me, treating children in a manner that can lead to the creation of more lost souls in this world is a crime against humanity.

More parents need to realize that harsh demands for cooperation in the name of obedience represent nothing more than a need for control... a misbegotten need which lends itself to the destruction of any desire for true cooperation on the part of the child. It should not be difficult to observe that kids do not like being ordered about and told what to do any more than we do, especially by loved ones. It's hurtful for us, and it's hurtful for kids. The hurt leads to anger, the anger leads to resentment, and the resentment leads to willful disobedience.

Consequences

I believe that all *imposed* consequences serve as punishment. Children don't need to learn that there are consequences to their actions and behavior... young kids learn that lesson on their own on a daily basis. For example, when a youngster breaks a favorite toy, they suffer an upsetting consequence and learn to take greater care in the future.

When we allow children the freedom to make decisions on their own (with our guidance, when needed), they not only develop their decision-making skills, they also learn to have confidence in their own judgment, and this serves to raise their level of self-esteem.

A measure of self-determination granted to children also serves to facilitate the development of 'inner-controls' as a guide to behavior, rather than a reliance on the 'external-controls' of punishments. One of A.S. Neill's biggest contributions to the practice of child rearing was the idea that *self-discipline comes from within, not from without.*

Children with a healthy level of self-esteem will tend to stand up for themselves and will be resistant to being bullied by adults. These are the children who make the least desirable targets for adults with ill intentions who would prefer the easier-to-manipulate obedient child. It's the confident, unbowed children who don't get into the stranger's car when told to, and they don't submissively allow unwanted advances by adults. I believe these factors better serve children than being taught to fear all strangers. As a society we tend to grow up in this world with a desire to socialize, yet carry an exaggerated fear of one another. These two behaviors are incongruent in terms of our ability to function socially on an optimally satisfactory level.

Having mentioned self-esteem, I should add that punishment often serves to reduce levels of self-esteem. Actually it's meant to, as the idea has always been to 'break' the offender of the behavior. The problem with this treatment is that it also tends to break the spirit of the child when the punishments are too severe and come too often for any given child. The danger lies in the fact that no one can know exactly when this point of spiritual damage might occur on an individual basis.

Many parents are overly concerned about their children getting too 'big a head', becoming a 'brat', becoming too independent, or getting too rebellious. Parents who hold these concepts should also be worrying about themselves in terms of getting stuck in a mindset of antiquated notions. When one looks at the two extremes of self-esteem, with helplessness and hopelessness at the low-end, and egocentrism on the high-end, it's not hard to see that a parent should err on the side of high self-esteem when it comes to meting-out negative discipline.

After all, low self-esteem is commonly associated with mental illness, anti-social behavior, addiction, homelessness, and all manner of other debilitating behaviors that prevent one from reaching their full potential in life. While, on the other hand, egocentrism is mainly associated with the development of personal problems of a social nature, and is often correlated with success, both in academics and chosen profession (with a distinction being made that might tend to exclude those persons who have been taught to feel superior to those around them).

It should also be pointed-out that those little tyrannical, obnoxious, spoiled brats are the products of permissive parents. These are typically dysfunctional parents who are actually fearful of ever upsetting their kids and subsequently allow them to infringe upon the rights of others in an effort to keep the peace. Rest assured, this type of parent is rare, indeed (more on this topic later).

I believe that an inherent problem with the relatively new concept of 'consequences' being adopted in lieu of punishments, is the tendency for parents to simply use consequences as a euphemism for punishment, as in, 'I don't punish my child, I use consequences'. In the same euphemistic way, some parents say, 'I don't hit my children, I only spank them'.

It's perfectly understandable that parents are concerned about preparing their children for the outside world. Sadly, some parents prepare their kids by exposing them to pain because there's pain 'out there'; some might create stress for their children because there's stress 'out there'; some might even inflict violence upon their children because there's violence and cruelty 'out there'.

In truth, this time-honored 'toughen 'em up' Spartan approach to child rearing is wholly counter-productive. A widely misunderstood idea is philosopher Fredrick Nietzsche's assertion that if something doesn't kill us, it makes us stronger. If this often quoted notion were true, mental institutions would be far and few in-between, mental health workers would be filing for bankruptcy, people would be asking, 'What's a rehab center?', and fewer people would be making their home out of a cardboard box in some back-alley.

Now, let's see what we get from a more current, up-to-date formula for strength and toughness:

Love and Acceptance → Self-Esteem → Stress Tolerance

This might seem a bit abstract, but this formula is easily tested by anyone. One need only ask themselves, 'When do things bother me the least?' In other words, 'When am I toughest, bravest, and strongest?' The answer is obvious... stressful situations bother us least when we are feeling good about ourselves, our lives, and our state of well-being. On the other hand, none of us are more susceptible to succumbing to stress (or 'losing it') than when we are feeling badly about ourselves or feeling helpless or hopeless.

So, I think it's safe to say that negative interaction with our children cannot be positive, and positive interaction with our children cannot be negative... at least in terms of parents preparing their children for later life out there in the world. Many talk of a need for adults to take responsibility for their actions regardless of their upbringings, but sadly, many children are never provided the opportunity to develop into responsible adults. I am not alone in suggesting that negative/punitive methods of parental discipline serve as a major factor.

PUNISHMENT AS A BELIEF

As a society, we know that punishment is a poor deterrent to unacceptable behavior unless the punisher is constantly on the scene. Our primary excuse for punishment is to teach (as in 'teach a lesson', or 'you *will* learn not to do that'), yet we all know that coercion and punishment in a learning environment does not a good teacher make.

Regardless, in our rush to judge and punish, we make our children become liars and sneaks, and we teach our criminals to do a better job of not getting caught the next time they commit a crime. The fear of getting caught becomes the primary concern of the wrongdoer. It's an orientation to external behavioral control rather than the self-discipline of internal control.

As with animals, putting humans in a cage runs a high risk of producing dysfunctional behavior. Yet, we continue to place victimless offenders behind bars. Some cultures see us as being enamored with punishment. Truth is, most of us don't love to punish. Our penchant for punishment is simply one part of a belief system that we adopt within a punitive home environment during our formative years.

We also know that criminals tend to come out of prisons more anti-social than when they went in. But, our blind commitment to the concept of punishment allows us to overlook the policies and practices of a largely ineffective penal system. It's not hard to suppose that retribution and vengeance under the guise of 'justice' plays a part in our thinking. I think we can agree that there are those criminals who pose a violent threat to society and need to be kept segregated. Truth is, such offenders represent only a small percentage of our prison population.

Our beliefs related to punishment defy logic. We see a public outcry against the early releases of prisoners, and the rationale behind these outcries holds that we don't want more criminals out on the streets in spite of the fact that these offenders *will* nevertheless be released at some point in time. As a largely Christian nation, we can only surmise that the passage of scripture, *Vengeance is mine, sayeth the Lord*, has been interpreted as an endorsement of 'vengeance for all'. It would even seem that we welcome it. After all, Christianity is the driving force behind the desire to have unwanted babies born into the world and then execute them or imprison them when they don't turn out to be good citizens as adults.

The concept of offenders making restitution to their victims is a seldom-discussed form of justice, and we are certainly more in favor of making inmates suffer than we are in rehabilitating them. We maintain the notion that punitive suffering will deter future anti-social behavior even though it's commonly known that the majority of parolees will wind up back in prison. It's almost as if we, as a society, have a *need* for punishment'.

Is it any wonder that we are so bent on punishing our children? And, what tragic irony it is that the children raised in punitive, authoritarian homes become the most likely candidates to be punished by society at a later time, both lawfully and socially.

DAMAGED SPIRITS AND FAILED POTENTIAL

People wonder what's wrong with hitting kids when so many kids are hit by their parents, but still turn out 'just as normal' as anyone else. The problem is... our standards of normal behavior are below what they could be. For example, it's not uncommon for neurotic people to say that they 'turned-out just fine' in comparison to what can normally be expected from other members of society. A team of Sociologists (Putney and Putney) has termed this phenomenon, 'Normal Neurosis'.

We know full well that there is more involved with being able to lead a happy, gratifying life than exceptional intelligence, or being born into money. Yet, it seems as if the notion persists that we're simply born with varying degrees of potential. Consequently, when we are led to believe that we are born deficient (in the absence of organic brain damage), we are willing to settle for being viewed as typical, hard-working, law-abiding, average citizens. Some of us even settle for careers consisting of menial labor because we have come to see ourselves as being incapable of anything requiring a greater level of skill or education.

This perception doesn't merely point to failed potential, it points to failed humanity... failed humanity in the sense that too many of us are robbed of the opportunity (or sufficient nurturing) to develop adequate levels of self-esteem... even to the extent that our society can view failed human potential as 'normality'. While there may be other reasons for failed potential, this reason should head the list of likely possibilities. After all, there is no reason to believe that innate levels of intelligence differ significantly between the opposite ends of the spectrum: organic brain damage and genius. I.Q. tests are more a measure of previous learning than they are of 'learning potential'.

I would submit that because of the ways children are treated in our culture, they wind up as adults that are willing to settle for much less than what they may have once wished for in life during earlier times. We diminish children, we erode their spirits, and we chip-away at their human potential... all in the name of parental righteousness or 'raising them up right'. As a consequence, our culture has come to consider it as normal behavior when we grow into adults who exhibit some of the following behaviors:

1. We develop a fear of speaking to a group of strangers. This represents a fear so commonly held on our part that it is generally considered to fall within the range of 'normal' behavior. Yet, this fear of others would seem unnatural in light of the fact that we inherently possess a need and desire to interact with others.

2. We learn to view 'eye for an eye' punishments as acceptable, while avoiding the words 'vengeance' or 'retribution'. This is a conventional normal view, which we continue to hold regardless of the fact that it flies in the face of what we have learned in recent times about human behavior as it relates to criminal acts. As a society, we know that criminal offenders are typically released from prisons more anti-social than when they went in... yet we insist on our 'pound of flesh' even at the risk of creating people who will become a greater danger to us.

3. We commonly beat ourselves up over the fact that we too often behave in ways that are less acceptable to us than what we would like. This is very normal behavior for most of us, yet it shouts of irrationality. Guilt-ridden individuals seldom possess adequate levels of self-esteem.

4. We use illicit, prescribed, or legal drugs to help us cope with the stresses of day-to-day life. The phrase, 'I could use a drink' is normally found acceptable, and sometimes even met with nods of understanding approval.

5. We come to view violence toward children as something different from violence toward adults... just as it was once 'normal' to view violence toward women as something different from violence toward men.

6. We wind up introducing jealousy into committed relationships, which then results in behavior on our part that serves to jeopardize those very relationships we want so much to maintain. This would have to be considered irrational behavior by any definition, but it is nevertheless, very normal behavior related to what we generally consider to be abnormal behavior.

7. We can look upon those who suffer misfortune, deprivation, or sub-standard abilities, with a lack of compassion or tolerance. For example, it is normal for us to walk past homeless people as if they, along with the whole issue of homelessness, simply did not exist. It is also quite normal for us to eschew compas-

sion by looking upon those feeling helpless and hopeless, as people who are nothing more than lazy. We look for excuses to not care. This relates to the fact that our commonly seen failure to reach the level of emotional development, which includes altruistic tendencies, falls well within the spectrum of what we consider 'normal' behavior within our society.

Some might claim that it is the abusive treatment of children (spankings which leave marks) that bears the responsibility for the creation of anti-social, violent, mentally disturbed, suicidal, and otherwise maladapted young people being introduced into society... but these more severely damaged people represent the extreme consequences of harsh upbringings and are not the focus of this chapter.

The people to whom I've been referring are those of us who have suffered less damage, and 'turned-out just fine' according to the norms of society. It shouldn't be difficult to deduce that what can be called the 'normal, turned-out-fine neurosis' is a product of less severe punitive measures (as in non-injurious spankings) in conjunction with the punitive parental attitude toward children that allows for children to be struck in the first place. The attitude factor is significant because if parents are capable of diminishing the spirits of their children through treating them with varying degrees of violence, they are also very capable of inflicting other demeaning, emotionally damaging treatments upon their children in addition to hitting them. Acts of physical aggression against children represent the most effective way to cause spiritual diminishment, feelings of rejection, and reduced levels of self-esteem.

Through child rearing practices that subject us to physical punishments, we very often find ourselves struggling to overcome the emotional damage of anger, self-doubt, and low self-esteem. Sometimes we even prevail. But regardless, we are nevertheless forced to ask ourselves how much of our human potential has been taken from us as the result of growing up in an environment where we are too often treated with disrespectful, demeaning punishments and castigation. After all, these kinds of treatments are well known to leave even us adults feeling unworthy, inadequate, incompetent, and looked-down upon in lowly regard.

While many of us who were raised in such an environment might claim to have turned-out just fine, very few of us can honestly claim to possess the amount of self-esteem we would wish for ourselves, and even fewer of us are wholly satisfied with who we are, in spite of our best efforts.

We are, in the end, left with the question of what it is in our lives that prevents us from becoming the people we would like to become. Too many of us do or say things we later regret, but nevertheless find ourselves helpless to prevent the same behavior from repeatedly reoccurring; too many of us lack confidence, but can't seem to do anything about it; and, too many of us find ourselves overly stressed without the ability to resolve our problems in constructive ways... we instead swallow a pill, take a drink, pound on the kids, berate our spouses, perhaps join a cult, or even begin to explore the best methods of doing away with ourselves.

We all have dreams of finding success, happiness, and even greatness in our journey through life... I would suggest it is much more than a simple matter of genetics that causes us to find ourselves falling short of those dreams.

It is not unreasonable to consider that the practice of routine punishment of children can serve as a means of personal diminishment that can contribute to the development of diminished goals, surrendered dreams, and failed potential. Could it be that our parental practice of holding children to a lower standard of treatment might stand as one of the reasons why so many of us fail to eventually find ourselves having become 'all that we can be'?

Adult Anger

Because it's generally agreed that anger is invariably the cause of violent behavior, I thought it might be a good idea to talk about some lesser-considered aspects of anger as it relates to behavior.

There are only two personality types who can engage in violent behavior without the motivation of anger... the sadist and the sociopath. Those of us who have experienced a relatively normal socialization process need anger (or fear) to behave in a violent manner. We need to feel justified to behave violently, and we use the anger of being personally affronted or offended as a motivation.

We normally feel ugly when striking-out at another and, as things go, the way we feel is the way we look. All the beautiful features and make-up in the world cannot hide the ugly face of a mother in the act of striking her child.

But there is more to this anger business than just violence. We become irrational under the influence of anger. We say things to loved ones in anger that remain said forever... hurtful things never forgotten, and often never forgiven. We make decisions and choices under the influence of anger that many of us regret for the rest of our lives. And we find that too much anger can also take a toll on our bodies by way of psychosomatic disorders.

It's my opinion that the amount of anger we experience is related to the amount of abusive treatment we've been exposed to in our lives (not necessarily abusive in a legal sense. I am applying the word 'abusive' to an equal standard for all human beings, not just adults).

Two factors seem to play a significant role in the frequency and intensity of angry feelings developing in a person: self-esteem, and understanding. If we cannot increase the level of our self-esteem, we can at least do our best to develop as much understanding of those things that trigger our anger as we possibly can.

As a personal example, I've had to explore the possible reasons why people drive in a dangerous or inconsiderate manner. By understanding the various reasons why people drive as recklessly as they do, I can view the anger I experience as a result of my own shortcomings. This insight reduces the likelihood that I would become a perpetrator of road rage, and behaving in a dangerous, irrational manner.

This education in developing a greater understanding also holds true for the way in which we react to the behavior of children. While none of us are beyond the experience of frustration → fear → anger, we can reduce the frequency and intensity of the anger we experience through a greater knowledge and understanding as to why children behave as they do.

In terms of children, the best example I can think of involves a parent feeling affronted by a child who is reacting in anger as a result of feeling hurt, unloved, or rejected by a parent. A parent who might lack an awareness of this possibility might instead consider this reaction by the child to represent nothing more than disobedience, disrespect, or defiance.

I've never met anyone who enjoyed the experience of anger. I've never met a child who enjoyed being treated in an angry, hateful manner. We need to be ever vigilant of the fact that we are never more prone to irrational behavior than when we are angry. If it is possible to consider the great majority of our anger to be the result of our own shortcomings, we can then consider that acting on that anger might be unjustifiable. After all, we so often come to regret acting in anger, do we not?

THE AUTHORITARIAN PERSONALITY

When giving consideration to the type of parent most likely to punish, and otherwise bully their children, it's important to define the 'Authoritarian Personality'. In order to do this, it would only be fair to consider the definition of this behavioral pattern provided by the man who coined the term in 1950 (Theodor W. Adorno).

The following is a paraphrased description of authoritarian characteristics. This list is based on the classic work, *The Authoritarian Personality*, (by Adorno, Frenkel-Brunswick, Levinson & Sanford):

'1. Rigid, unthinking adherence to conventional, middle-class ideas of right and wrong. The distinction has to be made between (a) incorporating universal values and (b) having blind allegiance to traditional social-political-religious customs or organizations. Examples: an egalitarian person who truly values one-person-one-vote, equal rights, equal opportunities, and freedom of speech will support a democracy, not a dictatorship. A person who says, 'I love my country--right or wrong' or 'America--love it or leave it' may be a flag-waving, patriotic speech-making politician who is secretly an antidemocratic authoritarian. For the authoritarian the values of respecting and caring for others are not as important as being a 'good German' or a 'good American' or a 'good Catholic' or a 'good Baptist'.

Important values to an authoritarian are obedience, cleanliness, success, inhibition or denial of emotions (especially anger and even love), firm discipline, honoring parents and leaders, and abhorring all immoral sexual feelings. Authoritarian parents tend to produce dominated children who become authoritarian parents. Egalitarians produce egalitarians.

2. Respect for and submission to authority--parents, teachers, religion, bosses, or any leader. This includes a desire for a strong leader and for followers to revere the leader, following him (seldom her) blindly. It was believed by the psychoanalytic writers of The Authoritarian Personality that recognizing one's

hostile feelings towards an authority was so frightening that the authoritarian personality was compelled to be submissive. There is an emphasis on following rules and regulations, on law and order. Everyone has a proper role to play, including gender role.

3. They take their anger out on someone safe. In an authoritarian environment (family, religion, school, peer group, government), the compliant, subservient, unquestioning follower stores up unexpressed anger at the authority. The hostility can't be expressed towards the authority, however, so it is displaced to an outsider who is different--a scapegoat. Unconsciously, the authoritarian says, 'I don't hate my father; I hate Jews (or blacks or unions or management or ambitious women or Communists or people on welfare)'. The 'good cause' to which one is dedicated often dictates who to hate, who to be prejudice against.

4. They can't trust people. They believe 'people who are different are no good.' If we believe others are as bad or worse than we are, we feel less guilt: 'Everybody looks out for #1' or 'Everybody would cheat if they had a chance.' Such a negative view of people leads to the conclusion that harsh laws and a strong police or army are necessary. Also, it leads people to foolishly believe that humans would 'go wild' and be totally immoral if they lost their religion.

5. Because they feel weak, authoritarian personalities believe it is important to have a powerful leader and to be part of a powerful group. Thus, they relish being in the 'strongest nation on earth,' the 'master race,' the 'world-wide communist movement,' 'the wealthiest nation,' the 'best corporation,' the 'best part of town,' the 'best-looking crowd,' the 'best team,' etc. The successful, the powerful, the leaders are to be held in awe. And the authoritarian says, 'When I get power, I want to be held in awe too. I'll expect respect, just like I demand it from my children.'

6. Over-simplified thinking. If our great leaders and our enormous government tell us what to do, if our God and our religion direct our lives, then we don't have to take responsibility for thinking or deciding. We just do what we are told. And, in general, we, 'the masses,' are given simple explanations and told the solutions are simple by authoritarian leaders. Examples:

'The source of the trouble is lenient parents (or schools or laws),' 'God is on our side,' 'Get rid of the Jews (or Capitalists or Communists or blacks or Arabs).' For the authoritarian if things aren't simple, they are unknowable, e.g., he/she endorses the statement, 'science has its place, but there are many important things that can never possibly be understood by the human mind.'

7. Guard against dangerous ideas. Since the authoritarian already has a handle on the truth, he/she opposes new ideas, unconventional solutions, and creative imaginations. They believe an original thinker is dangerous; he/she will think differently. It's considered good to be suspicious of psychologists, writers, and artists who probe your mind and feelings--such people are scary. Governments who observe subversives are OK, though. Indeed, censorship of the media may become necessary, especially if the media becomes critical of our leaders or sexually provocative. A businessperson produces needed products; an intellectual is a threat.

8. Ethnocentrism: Everything of mine is better than yours--my country, my religion, my kind of people, my family, and my self. Research has also shown the authoritarian is more prejudiced and more prone to punish people (including their own children) to get them to work harder or to do 'right' (Byrne & Kelley).'

AUTHORITY AND IMPOSITION

Does authority need to be intimidating?

Sure enough, we sometimes have to impose ourselves on our children. After all, they can't understand that the painful shot they're getting from this scary stranger wearing a white coat is for their 'own good'. The question is how do we exert our 'authority/control' over a confused, misunderstanding young child? Should we intimidate them with a harsh demand of 'You *will* do this!' or should we commiserate with compassion and empathy so that they can at least know that we're on their side?

I love the Christian 'golden rule' that states you should do unto others as you would have them do unto you. But, because kids are still trying to learn what this world is all about, in addition to all those things that are expected of them, children are left in a position that requires us, as parents to give *more* unto them as 'others' than we should expect to have done unto us.

In other words, if *we* complain about having to get an injection from the doctor, we might not feel putout by hearing something said like, 'Oh stop it, you know you have to get this shot... just do it'. We might even tolerate being laughed at a little for being so silly. We've been around long enough to understand. Thing is, young kids do *not* understand in the beginning. Consequently, if we are going to be caring, concerned parents, we should be more respectful and sensitive toward our children when they are confronted with these kinds of situations.

When it comes to imposing ourselves upon our kids it becomes a matter of degree and frequency. Perhaps it's because we all know that kids tend to emulate us, please us, and cooperate with our wishes, that we sometimes take them for granted or take advantage of their willingness to quickly forgive our harshness or rudeness toward them.

Children being ordered about to perform tasks or errands that serve the self-interest of only the parent is a good example of imposition. These kinds of demands made upon them can make them feel as if they are being placed in the role of an indentured servant (it hurts their feelings to be told what to do just as it usually hurts our feelings to be 'ordered about' rather than 'respectfully requested'). Because parents often interpret these kinds of angry 'hurt feelings' reactions to represent displays of defiance from the child, many will react by introducing a level of intimidation to coerce the child into compliance. In using intimidation as a means of control, a parent might demand that the children pick-up their toys, while the kids are wondering why mom is being mean and hurtful (with anger and resistance a common reaction).

The kids are left to draw this conclusion because it makes no sense at all to young children to pick-up all their toys when they are just going to be playing with them again later. In circumstances such as these (which often apply where young children are concerned), is it really a good idea to impose our authority upon children with harsh demands and the threat of punishment? I don't think so. But, as an alternate approach to negative discipline, the kids might very well respond positively if the parent were to instead make a worried fuss over being afraid of tripping over a toy and getting hurt. This 'teaching' tact is worlds apart from imposing intimidating threats because instead of the children feeling unfairly treated and hurt they are presented with the undesirable prospect of their toys possibly hurting a family member. As a result, they will be much more prone to offer their willing cooperation in picking-up their toys. Seeking the cooperation of children is far superior to demanding it, while serving as an approach that poses no risk to the quality of the parent-child relationship.

It's simply a myth that parents are required to sacrifice a high quality human relationship with their children in the name of maintaining control over them through intimidation, threat, and punitive measures. I can't imagine a more important human relationship for pursuing a respectful, mutually nurturing, harmonious, high-quality relationship, than the one between parent and child. But instead, it seems that on the contrary, many parents can be seen showing more consideration, regard, and respect toward another adult, like the cashier at the supermarket who's a complete stranger, than the parent shows toward their own children. I wonder if anyone has failed to personally observe this phenomena taking place.

What's sad about this is the fact that our keeping a distant 'air of authority' over our children is not only illusionary in terms of the best way to stay in control, it's also entirely unnecessary and often counterproductive in terms of the desired outcome. The kids sure aren't impressed with our power issues and our assumed notions that intimidation is the only avenue by which to gain their cooperation. And, they're more likely to hurtfully resent being treated with such rude, disrespectful regard.

We all know as parents that from very early on, our own day-to-day behavior is a behavioral *model* for our kids, and they do their best to emulate what we do. If the word 'please' is in our vocabulary, our kids learn the word 'please'. If we relate to our children in a respectful manner, they learn to relate to us in a respectful manner. However, if we make our wishes known by demanding, 'You *will* do this, and you *will* do that', in the form of warnings, we can fully expect that our kids will be prone to making their own wishes known to others in the same rude manner they have learned from us.

This modeling process works very well as a learning tool for children until we begin to lose patience with them by expecting that they should learn what we are teaching them at a faster pace than is reasonable. This usually applies to the rules and regulations we expect them to adopt and internalize. For example, manners and social graces are extremely difficult socialization skills for kids to learn. It's not unreasonable for a young child to ask, 'Mommy, what do the words 'please' and 'thank you' have to do with me asking to play outside? And, it doesn't make sense to me when *you* don't use those words when you ask *me* to put on those stupid hot clothes and shoes before we go out on a hot day in Summer'.

I give these examples because part of the problem with parents losing their patience as good teachers comes through their having long forgotten the level of logic available to young children. Too often, because of our inability to relate to the world through the eyes of our children, we look through our own eyes and see many of the lessons we've already learned as amazingly simple things that have long been mere matters of a second nature to us.

This perception can lead us to feel that the children must not wish to listen, or cooperate, or show proper respect, or are displaying disobedience, when they keep breaking rules 'they have already learned, and they should now know better'. It's often at this point in the relationships we have with our children that we first begin to lose patience with them and become more demanding and punitive. The question is, are they failing us, or are we failing them? When we as parents fail them, most kids will blame themselves for failing to meet parental expectations.

But, given the possible circumstances that I touched upon above, many might find it a highly beneficial exercise to take another look at one of our more time-honored parenting concepts. Of course, I'm referring to a parenting practice of discipline that is built upon a counter-nurturing foundation of imposition, subjugation, intimidation, and coercion. And, if we can no longer see the world through the eyes of a young child, are we justified in subjecting our children to these unloving forms of treatment in the face of our inability to understand why they do the things they do? And, would we consider it an act of cruelty to inflict punishment upon a child based on a mistaken assumption on our part through a lack of thorough understanding as to the actual reasons behind the behavior being punished?

I say 'we' because there was a time early on in my adult life when I shared this authoritarian attitude toward children myself. I went on to discover that the more I learned about child behavior, the more I found the concept of punishment, as so many parents apply it, to be unfair, unnecessary, and the cause of a great deal of unjust suffering on the part of children.

I recently saw someone quoting a statement saying that 'we get angry at our kids because we can'. I'm forced to add that we also sometimes bully our kids because we can. Then again, we certainly can't be expected to be perfect human beings or mistake-proof parents, but, at least when it comes to our kids, we can strive for perfection.

PARENTS AS FRIENDS

Question: How do we characterize the relationship that most parents have with their children in human terms? Are they friends, acquaintances, enemies, or perhaps virtual strangers, living together in the same household? I'd suggest that we don't commonly consider children to be worthy of friendship.

It should be a reasonable question to ask why it is that so many parents feel that children are the only segment of humanity that is worthy of being generally treated in a disrespectful and demeaning manner. Perhaps part of the problem stems from parents taking advantage of the fact that kids are so quick to forgive a parent for treating them in crass, insensitive ways... many kids even come to feel *deserving* of being treated as lesser beings who represent a lesser value in this world. I'd like to have a dollar for every time I've seen a parent cordially smiling at an adult, suddenly turn to snarl at their child for whatever reason, then turn back to the adult again with a warm friendly smile as if they had just suffered a schizophrenic episodic break from reality.

We don't threaten our friends with violence to get our own way, or glare menacingly at them as a warning of impending violence as a means of intimidation. We take care not to dismiss what our friends have to say. It's very rude to do so. We don't physically punish friends to correct their undesired behavior, or to gain a measure of retribution for having offended us. And we don't hit our friends as a display of our caring, or as a means of getting them to do what we want them to do.

Some might say that, unlike the parent-child relationship, one is not responsible for the welfare of friends. I would disagree. Others might say that while children need discipline, friends do not. Not true. In establishing successful relationships we define the parameters of what behaviors are acceptable to us. In doing so, we discipline (teach) the other person as to how the relationship might succeed. For example, we verbally correct the other person when they engage in behavior that is unacceptable to us. Others yet might argue that a student-teacher relationship cannot involve friendship. Again, I would disagree. Many successful friendships involve one party taking a leadership role in the relationship.

The level of esteem (respect) in which we are willing to hold another depends on how we view that other person. If we are of a mind that the other person is not worthy of our consideration or esteem, we either avoid them, or treat them rudely. I think everyone would have to agree that kids are much more prone than adults to being treated rudely. As a matter of fact, most of us would probably be hard-put to remember the last time we heard an adult refer to a child as having been treated rudely... kids are rarely afforded such considerations.

It seems to me that parents should strive to be the best of friends with their children because parents are in a position to be the most important friend their children would ever have. In friendship, a parent serves in the role of a trusted, supportive confidant who possesses a great deal of wisdom to share and impart about the more important aspects of everyday life. It's a tragedy to me that so many parents emotionally drive their children away because they are under the misguided illusion that they at times need to treat their children as adversaries. We adults are quick to lose trust, become closed-off emotionally, and are less apt to communicate openly with a friend who would hit us, or otherwise treat us in ways that clearly indicate that they have little regard for our feelings or worth. It's certainly no different for children.

I'm defining 'friend' in the broadest sense, without stipulations or conditions... a relationship consisting of love, respect, honor, warmth, and open communication. I think it's sadly ironic that parents would choose to deny friendship to their kids in light of the fact that kids desperately need and want little more than the very friendship they are being denied.

Given the relatively recent establishment of Positive Discipline as a more effective means of discipline than the traditional punitive approaches, perhaps we, as a society, will begin to entertain the possibility that adults can establish genuine friendships with children. Before laughing at such a notion, we should keep in mind that just 50 years ago, many men would be quick to laugh at the notion of women being considered friends. Beyond that, men generally viewed the women of less than a century ago as being in need of a strong, guiding hand in their lives. Husbands were willing to take on this disciplinary responsibility, just as many parents today make the claim that they have a responsibility to treat their children in a disrespectful, demeaning manner in the name of a strong, guiding hand... a position that destroys any possibility of establishing a friendly relationship in the true sense of the word. It's truly ironic that many women of today deny their children that which they were once commonly denied as a gender... the invaluable concept of friendship with a loved one.

Children are people too. And, as such, they are as deserving of loving friendship as the rest of us. Friendship is not a different matter when it comes to children any more than it's a different matter for any of us who come from varying worlds of perception, education, or level of development.

SPOILED SCHMOILED

It seems to me that an important consideration related to the ways in which we treat our children involves the inexplicable notion held by many parents that without punitive discipline, kids will become those dreaded 'spoiled brats'. And there it is, the term that serves to strike fear in the hearts of so many parents.

Probably the most common definition associated with spoiling children involves an idea that sees 'parents giving their kids whatever they want'. Unfortunately, many parents are under the impression that this parents-giving-them-whatever-they-want concept refers to the physical needs and desires of children. On the other hand, some of these same parents tend to become very unclear when it comes to defining the emotional criteria for spoiling kids.

I recently heard a prominent basketball coach in an interview on TV say that, although he was sitting on a pile of money, he wasn't going to leave any of it to his children because it would just spoil them and ruin their lives. I know I'm citing an extreme example here to make my point, but this misguided man is a victim of society's myth about spoiling children. To this coach, cutting his kids out of his will is an act of love, strange as that may seem.

I think a good question to ask is, 'What actual good is born out of intentionally depriving children of wishes and desires merely for the sake of preventing them from becoming spoiled?' I would say none that makes any sense. As a matter of fact, there is probably no one who could reasonably explain the relationship between intentional deprivation and 'spoiling'. I submit that the two are entirely unrelated to one another. In addition, a child considered spoiled in a strictly physical sense will become an adult who many will tend to be described as an individual who is confident, determined, persistent, undefeatable, tireless, resourceful, dogged, and ambitious when it comes to obtaining what they desire on a physical level (money, home, car, etc.).

This type of behavior can result from an individual simply being relatively unaccustomed to being denied those things wished for or desired. These are often persons who may have very well come to believe that they possess an unalienable right to obtain whatever they desire so long as they expend the necessary amount of effort that will be required to achieve their goal (of course, we know this trait as 'ambition'). However, this personal drive does not necessarily mean, by any means, that such individuals will be willing to step all over other people for the sake of their own personal gain. Nor, for that matter, does it mean they would treat others in an obnoxious, inconsiderate, or otherwise disrespectful manner.

That leaves us with the emotional aspect of spoiling children as a matter to consider. We already know that one of the greatest fears of many parents is to have their kid wind up being perceived by others as being a spoiled brat in need of better discipline/parenting. Traditionally, children who have been described in such a way, have not only been considered unacceptable socially, they were viewed in such a negative light that it wouldn't be much of a stretch to consider such children as violating a social taboo. This is why the truly obnoxious spoiled brat is an exception to the rule in our society (and, for that matter, the known world). Truth is, society does anything but spoil children with overindulged rights and protections.

So, what conditions then create the development of an insufferable, obnoxious, spoiled little brat? A.S. Neill of *Summerhill* fame had only one golden rule that was strictly enforced in his school, the rule stated that *children are not permitted to infringe on the rights of others.* The students enrolled in this school were granted the freedom to experiment with their own rules and regulations as a means of having them live and learn how to function within a democratic process. However, his golden rule was the only one he insisted remain in place as a permanent, non-negotiable rule. Initially aghast over the thought of wild little spoiled brats running a whole school, I spent over a year researching the conditions and consequences of such a relatively free environment for children. Follow-up studies on Summerhill graduates generally showed these young adults to be exceptionally well adjusted, fully functioning individuals possessed of uncommonly high levels of social-skill development. Notably, none of these former students were reported to exhibit behavior that would be consistent with any of the characteristics that are commonly associated with spoiled behavior.

In essence, A.S. Neill made this question of overindulging children an amazingly simple one. His position held that if you gave kids complete freedom, you would turnout little despotic tyrants. But, give kids love, respect, and a healthy consideration for the rights of others, and you'll turn out happy, well-adjusted little beauties.

It would be easy for anyone to claim that the latter statement is grossly simplistic. I would agree were it not for my own personal experience and years of observation.

I can still remember a time when I was constantly being warned that the way I was raising my kids was going to turn them into insufferable little brats. The warnings started over 35 years ago, and slowly decreased over time as it became increasingly apparent to any observer that my kids would have to be described as anything but spoiled. From their earliest days, the behavior of my children has represented a contradiction to generally held definitions of spoiled. It's been my experience that little tyrants are created by that rare, dysfunctional parent who actually fears the prospect of upsetting their kids, and are consequently prone to tolerate any and all behavior exhibited by the kids (more on this topic in the following chapter).

I feel concern and compassion for that little despotic spoiled brat that comes along now and then. These are children who are susceptible to experience a significant degree of social difficulties. But, the problems laying in wait for the spoiled child pale in comparison to the myriad of possible debilitating emotional maladies that may lie ahead for the child who falls at the other end of the behavioral spectrum. We, as a society, should be making more strident attempts to inform the public that the child at most risk to suffer a disordered existence is the child who sits quietly in the corner while displaying a degree of fearfulness and emotional distance.

Traditionally, we've liked these quiet, compliant kids who were actually encouraged by societal standards to be 'seen and not heard'. It might be time for us to wake up to the fact that the risks to the wellbeing of children are associated to a much greater degree with the behavioral characteristics of those quite, seemingly respectful (but actually fearful), compliant kids. Kids who are much more likely to suffer emotional difficulties related to low self-esteem, alienation, depression, emotional disorders, substance addiction, failed potential, and suicide. I would strongly suggest that the numbers of spoiled children who wind up in rehabilitation programs, mental hospitals, homeless shelters, and prisons would pale in comparison to those raised in authoritarian home environments.

It seems to me that it might be a good time for us to focus more of our worries and fears in the direction of those kids on the authoritarian end of the spectrum who are being raised in ways that serve to rob them of adequate self-esteem, while being deprived of an opportunity for healthy emotional growth and development.

It's been my experience that the prevalence of spoiled children is largely insignificant in comparison to the prevalence of children treated in a sufficiently harsh manner as to cause long term emotional damage, and psychological problems.

I believe that most parents know in their hearts that what their children really need is huge amounts of love, affection, caring, warmth, support, encouragement, praise, and laughter. The dreaded word 'spoiled' needs to be kept in context! How many parents reading this would actually consider letting little sister get beat-on by their big brother, or letting the kids use the new furniture as a trampoline, or allowing unimportant interruptions while taking an important phone call? Nary a soul, I would venture. Not permitting this type of behavior is what prevents spoiling. So I'd like to suggest that parents concentrate on that good, positive nurturing that we all really want, and put aside any excessive concerns about the contrived, mistaken rules of society which would have us treat our kids in a punitive, negative manner for the sake of obsolete tradition.

PERMISSIVE PARENTING

'Permissiveness' should only be a concern for parents who find themselves generally intimidated by their children, and consequently find themselves allowing the children to engage in virtually any and all behavior. These are parents who are emotionally ill-equipped to cope with negative emotions through a fear of being exposed to upset and distress.

I see two major risks involved with this rare type of dysfunctional parenting (which is not a formalized approach toward child rearing): 1. The truly permissive parent will sometimes choose to simply remove the child from danger without attempting to teach the child a fear of the danger involved. 2. Besides increased physical risk, the most significant danger involves the parent failing to properly socialize the child according to the norms and values of society, which mainly involves the parent failing to teach the child that infringing upon the rights of others is unacceptable.

A child who is failed by their parents in this regard becomes the little obnoxious, despotic, tyrannical, 'spoiled brat' type of child who parents so fear producing. It has come to the point that being perceived as having created a spoiled brat can be considered a social taboo. I think it helps for people to understand that permissive parents do not have a handbook on 'How to Be Permissive', nor do they ever intend to produce a little tyrant.

Some parents worry about being permissive, but unless they happen to be a parent who allows their child to infringe upon the rights of others (or their own) through a fear of upsetting them, or allows their child to engage in virtually any and all behavior in order to avoid the possibility of emotional upset, there's really not a whole lot to worry about. The personality traits I see associated with this type of parent are low self-esteem, extreme timidity, painful shyness, and submissiveness to the point of allowing the child to have control over the parent's better judgment.

What some parents might regard as permissive moments might be just as well regarded as a show of flexibility or a fair reconsideration. These parental behaviors do not a permissive parent make... nor does permissiveness relate to parents who have chosen to employ more enlightened (and more effective) non-violent, alternative methods of discipline in their approach toward child rearing.

And let me finish by adding that in my long experience, the prevalence of these types of parents is miniscule in proportion to the percentage of authoritarian parenting practices, which make up the vast majority of child rearing approaches in the U.S.

WHAT ABOUT PRAISE AND REWARDS?

My kids knew that I wanted to please them when I could, and they displayed a like desire to please me in turn (much in the same way as mutual respect becomes established). I can't stress enough how important it is for parents to have a clear understanding of the fact that children's natural propensity to please parents should not be perceived as children displaying behavior that could cause them to become 'praise dependent'. This view is an invalid notion that could cause parents to provide an un-nurturing response through a lack of enthusiasm and genuine sharing of the experience with the child. Such responses could eventually discourage children, with them finally giving-up on the idea of being able to generate a sharing of mutual enthusiasm and excitement with the parent. Unfortunately, the development of a decreased desire to please the parent creates the risk of causing there to be a reduction in the number of opportunities for meaningful, nurturing, positive interactions that occur between the parent and the child.

For example, a kid having cold water thrown on the joy and excitement of a new discovery, or newfound ability, by a largely restrained, subdued 'no praise' parent might say to themselves something like, 'I thought I did really well and even got all excited about it, but then mommy/daddy just gave me a lukewarm, dissatisfying response. Maybe I didn't do as well as I thought I did. Maybe I don't do as well as I think I do on other things, too'. Obviously, the risk here is that the child starts to develop some inner-doubts related to self-perception. Perhaps she/he comes to believe that they lack the ability to accurately evaluate the level of their abilities, competence, and maybe even their adequacy.

I have to say that praise makes us feel good because we possess a need for acceptance and approval, on both a social and familial level. True enough, it'd be nice at times if we could simply depend on ourselves without having to depend on others around us to reaffirm our value and worth in this world. But, unfortunately, we don't fare well in the absence of positive social interaction, social approval, and being recognized for our successes and contributions through social acclaim, or monetary gain as a *reward*.

As some might claim, I don't see us as having become dependent on praise as a result of having been praised throughout our childhoods to the extent that we become 'other-directed' (a total dependency on others for approval). I would suggest that a child who has gained a high level of self-esteem commonly associated with receiving approval, frequent praise, and recognized achievement, becomes an adult who exhibits a *lower* level of need for the approval of others and a lack of desire for total conformity.

I should also add that in my experience, maltreated children coming from abusive or neglectful homes display a much higher level of need for positive interaction than is typically seen in children. These often emotionally starved children are highly responsive to praise, approval, reward, acceptance, and being treated with a respect that provides them with an all-important sense of having worth and value in this world. There isn't any 'having grown dependent on praise' factor on the part of these kids... they are simply in greater need of feeling the love that comes through sincere, un-prescribed, unadulterated, praise/positive reinforcement, in *any* shape, form, or context.

On the other hand, the patronization of children doesn't sell for more than a minute. They seem to have a special knack for seeing through it. No one likes being constantly patronized, and some even develop distrust for sincere praise as a result (save those who dismiss sincerely offered words of praise as 'patronizing' as a result of their own low self-esteem).

I strongly suggest that loving relationships are built on mutual approval and high regard... a shared high level of esteem held by both parties toward one another, which becomes established largely through mutual expressions of praise. Most of us spend a good deal of our lives in a quest to find this blissfully unparalleled level of unquestioned approval and uncompromising acceptance, and we reach it through the highest level of praise being expressed in its purist, most concentrated form. It's a process that we know as 'falling in love'.

When it comes to praise, I've never heard of a ballplayer losing interest in their sport as a result of being continuously acknowledged and rewarded every time he scored a run or got a base hit. I've heard it said that the roar of the crowd alone can serve as a sufficient enough promise of reward to keep some players coming back for just one more year. Many players hang-on even if reaping those coveted rewards has by now become a much less likely probability.

Where children are concerned, the value of praise and rewards is much greater than it is for the ballplayer. There's certainly no doubt that children are often met with frustration and failure, as they struggle through such tasks as learning new motor skills or successfully achieving a desired goal. What a shame it would be for any parent to withhold praise or rewards that could be employed for the purpose of providing encouragement and support. Such offers of support can serve as very effective tools in helping the child get past those inevitable roadblocks along the way. This notion of withholding of praise would be an especially unfortunate shame if the parent remained silent as a result of having been sold on the idea that praise or reward will cause the child to lose interest in the activity in question.

I do agree with the position holding that it would be nice if more of us were less co-dependent, or other-directed. It is most certainly a self-esteem issue, and I think that the road to self-reliance, independence, and emotional strength is built on a deeply entrenched foundation of high self-esteem. This, to me, represents the most important beneficial aspect of 'Positive Discipline'. No doubt, it's an enlightened approach toward child rearing that provides an environment for children offering non-violent, non-coercive attitudes toward child rearing. For me, it's also an approach that should never fail to include unrestrained, enthusiastic, sincerely felt, expressions of love, approval, acceptance, encouragement, support, and confidence. These are the characteristics of any successful relationship, and I think it's important to note that they are feelings that are largely conveyed and established through spontaneous praise and various forms of reward. I realize this view tends to alarm some parents whose first priority is to prevent producing a 'spoiled brat', but such fears are largely unwarranted.

I'd also like to add that in my years of working with kids and parents in various professional capacities, I can say in all honesty that I've never encountered a child or adult who had been negatively effected on any level through having been called a 'good boy or girl', or a 'good man or woman'. Nor have I encountered anyone who displayed an over-dependence on winning praise from others as a basis for behavior resulting from early-on forms of praise or rewards. Nor, for that matter, anyone who possessed unrealistic self-expectations through being told too often that they were 'wonderful', 'terrific', and/or 'great'. I have also never encountered anyone who had suffered as a result of a parent gushing profusely over the beauty of their child's artistic endeavors, mastered skills, or successfully achieved goals and accomplishments.

The crime being committed on the part of these seemingly opportunistic proponents of 'harmful praise', and 'punishing rewards' isn't being perpetrated through the notions they promote, per se. No, the real crime is being committed through the confusion, fear, and uncertainty that these anti-praise theorists instill in parents, which come at the expense of the children's emotional needs being adequately satisfied. This circumstance offers an unacceptable level of risk. The potential for parents to find themselves silently avoiding offers of praise, while remaining unaware of the possibility that each subsequent instance of silence or seemingly cool indifference, could cause their child to suffer a mounting deprivation of needed confidence, timely encouragement, crucial support, affirmation, the nurture of positive interaction, or perhaps even the loss of a measure of self-esteem.

We should be focusing on the ways in which we can provide a home environment for our children that will serve to allow them to eventually reach their full potential as human beings and enable them to find joy and happiness in life.

SPANKING

INTRODUCTION

Many people, perhaps society as a whole, seem to believe that violence against others begins with portrayals of violence in the media, or music with violent lyrics, and/or those violent video games we hear so much about. Well, I'd like to suggest that violence begins in the home.

The striking of a child for punitive purposes represents an act of violence, regardless of the degree of violence inflicted.

It has been my experience that the most effective way to break the cycle of authoritarian parenting is to enlighten parents as to the possible risks associated with employing corporal punishment as a parenting practice. There now exists an overwhelming consensus within the professional and scientific communities against the practice of physically punishing children.

Following are a number of different reasons why the parenting practice of spanking children is an ill-advised method of negative discipline.

SPANKING FOR SAFETY IS A RISKY BUSINESS

I'd like to urge all parents to further ensure the safety of their children by teaching them to recognize danger on their own, without a need for anyone to stand by at close quarters on 24-hour-a-day watchdog duty. We've sold kids short by assuming that they are incapable of learning to avoid danger independently, and we've done so at their expense... a fact which is in evidence every time we see a toddler running onto a busy road.

Instead of acting as a mere external control, parents would better serve their children by simply conveying to them their own fear and avoidance of all that is dangerous. This parental conveyance enables children to internalize an awareness of the danger at hand... after all, this is how most living things quite effectively teach their young how to survive.

Unfortunately, the commonly seen teaching method used by human parents to teach safety issues, which could be called, 'The Yell and Hit Method of Teaching', is a most inefficient and harsh way to teach anything, let alone safety issues. As a matter of fact, this yell and hit approach is such a poor method of teaching that it can even prove to be counter-productive on occasion. It should be apparent that the major flaw in using anger and violence as a method of teaching kids to avoid danger lies in the looming prospect of the anger and violence causing the child to fear the parent rather than the actual danger at hand.

Let me explain a little about this 'conveyed fear' learning that we've left neglected and unnoticed for far too long now. It's probably safe to say that most parents are aware of the fact that even infants react instantaneously to the startled behavior of a parent. This is because babies are born into this world fully equipped to automatically shift into a survival mode of acute awareness in response to an alarm reaction on the part of the parent. As soon as the baby is capable of identifying a source of the parent's alarm, the baby will immediately adopt the same fear of the perceived threat as is held by the parent.

This ability of young children to immediately internalize the same fear displayed by a parent toward a source of danger is a built-in biological survival mechanism that parents should be utilizing to a much greater extent than we do at present. This inborn learning ability in children is biologically designed to act as an aid in helping our young learn how to avoid danger... and thereby enhance the probability of their survival. Most newborn animal species also share this inherent behaviorism. Except, unlike us, their parents take full advantage of its value in teaching survival skills to their young.

Additionally, we parents could save ourselves a great deal of worry and time by making use of this natural learning tool. It's a simple, yet proven technique that has over time shown itself to be much more effective, safe, and quick than other traditional, typically punitive, methods of teaching kids to avoid harm. This method utilizes the ability of children to internalize our conveyed fears and instantly adopt those fears as their own... and they do so in the form of a deeply ingrained learning process that can take mere minutes to stage and complete.

To illustrate how this method works, let's imagine that you are the parent of a toddler who is ready to learn to use caution when in the vicinity of moving vehicles. You might want to start by taking your toddler out by the roadside for the lesson during a period of light traffic. Begin to laugh and play while at the same time keeping an eye-out for that first vehicle to come along. When one comes into view, stiffen-up in alarm with a scared 'OH!', and point to the vehicle while making sure that your child is seeing the source of your alarm (rest assured that your child will be looking around for the cause of your distress). It only took one lesson to instill a sense of danger in my kids where moving vehicles are concerned, but if you see that your child is not wary of the road after the first teaching attempt, (perhaps through a failure to effectively convey your alarm) simply repeat the process until the message gets through. Few kids will remain immune to mom/dad jumping in startled alarm to a perceived threat.

Needless to say, this teaching method is highly effective for teaching children any and all safety issues. The hot stove is another commonly heard excuse given by parents for exacting punitive measures upon their children. But, there's a better, faster, and safer way for new parents to address this safety issue. First, turn your stove on to a high setting and let it get good and hot. Then go on a 'play crawl' with your (say 8-10 mo.) baby into the kitchen. Crawl close enough to the stove to feel the heat, then suddenly and abruptly stop dead with a vocalized alarm. You will have instantaneously gained the undivided attention of your baby. Slowly reach your hand out toward the hot stove until the level of heat becomes uncomfortable, then pull your hand back quickly with a wide-eyed start, while fearfully saying the word, 'Hot!' Baby might take-off beating a hasty retreat at that point, but may be just as likely to instead want to learn more about this danger by mimicking what you've just done by proceeding to slowly reach toward the stove themselves. Under a watchful eye, baby feels the same discomforting heat, and learns forever that a hot stove is best kept at a safe distance (of course, you will want to confirm this learning with follow-up observations under close supervision).

My daughter didn't actually have to reach-out to feel the heat because she crawled close enough to feel it and identify the stove as my source of alarm. On the other hand, my son cautiously reached-out to feel the discomforting heat just as I had done. Either way, both of my kids had internalized the desire to avoid getting too close to a hot stove from that point on. This process represents a safety lesson that can be permanently learned by a baby in as little as a minute's time. As a matter of fact, I've discovered that my method is so effective that it's better for parents to be under-dramatic and find that there's a need to repeat the exercise than it is to be over-dramatic and scare the heck out of poor baby. While fear is one of the least desirable or advisable emotions to instill in a child, there are nevertheless a few fears that they need to learn in order to survive.

My method involves a simple matter of some thought and creativity. Of course, childproofing is desirable, but it doesn't actually teach. For example, are all electrical outlets going to be covered in all places visited? Perhaps not. Crawl with baby to an outlet, stick a finger toward it, and then recoil in alarm. Crawl to the edge of steps with baby, and proceed to stop abruptly in alarm.

It's certainly understandable that a parent seeing their child placed in harms way is going to react with fear and alarm. I'd like to suggest that parents refrain from allowing their feelings of fear to develop into feelings of anger, at least where the teaching of safety issues is concerned. Anger leaves much to be desired as a teaching method, and is just as likely to motivate the child to simply avoid getting caught the next time (with the child being prone to come away thinking something along the lines of, 'I don't understand what was wrong with what I was doing, but for some mysterious reason it upsets mom, so I just won't do it when she's around'). Worse yet, young children have been known to begin running *away* from the alarmed, angry sounding shouts of a spanking parent through a fear of being hit. This reaction on the part of young children is especially risky near roads, parking lots, and swimming pools, where the danger lies ahead.

Any parent knows that there are moments, no matter how high the usual level of their vigilance, when young children are going to disappear from sight. One of the major purposes of this teaching method is to help address these potentially tragic instances by creating a greater degree of insurance against childhood accidental deaths and injuries. It's too often the case that children learn to avoid danger only in the presence of the punitive parent without an understanding of the actual risks associated with the behavior in question.

Mine is a method of teaching that serves to effectively hasten the process of children internalizing an independent ability to avoid danger, while also representing a means of teaching children without subjecting them to demeaning, disrespectful, or violent treatments.

Having said all that, I should also add that although this method of teaching safety issues is highly effective, it still doesn't replace the need for young children to be supervised at all times where the possibility of danger might exist.

NOTE: This approach may not show itself to be immediately effective in the absence of a well-functioning bond of trust between the child and the parent/caretaker. In such cases where there exists a degree of distrust, current acrimony, or alienation between the parent and child, repeated restaging of the lesson in question might be required.

THE EMOTIONAL CONSEQUENCES OF SPANKING

Those of us who are familiar with the public debate on spanking are aware of the need to stress a facet of spanking that seems to remain largely ignored by those in support of this practice... the high level of potential for negative short and long term emotional consequences.

Emotions are meant to carryout and protect our biological drives. But, it would seem apparent that many parents are unaware of the fact that emotions are an undeniable part of our biological make up.

This might help explain why it is we don't hear the term 'emotional beatings' being associated with the practice of spanking children nearly as often as we should. It's a term that too often gets overlooked in discussions related to physical punishment. One reason for this could stem from the fact that a great number of people would rather avoid conversations concerning 'emotional stuff'.

There are still a good number of people around who have developed a negative connotation with regard to the expression of emotions. It should seem clear that many of us still equate 'emotions' with 'weakness'. This could be due in part to the remnants of outdated patriarchal notions that cast a number of emotions in a negative light. For example, it's probably safe to say that no one likes a 'cry baby'; many of us view 'whiners' with contempt; some of us still regard the open expression of emotional distress as a 'lack of inner strength', while others of us yet find such expressions as downright pathetic, repulsive, and worthy of disdain.

This is probably why when we adults are emotionally distressed or hurting, we'll usually choose to blame our lack of desire to participate in work or play on a *physical* problem rather than admitting to an emotional difficulty. We don't usually call the boss to say that we're just 'not up' to coming into work that day because we are feeling stressed and need a day off, or that we're feeling 'down' and just don't feel like going in to work. Fact is, we're much more likely to call in sick *physically*, rather than chance being viewed as 'emotionally weak', 'unstable', or 'disturbed'.

This fear of appearing 'weak' or 'unstable' seems to leave many of us with a preference toward simply denying the negative emotional aspects of day-to-day living. There is no doubt that all of us can relate to emotional pain, yet we will often refuse to recognize it in others... especially in children.

Certainly, the commonly seen tendency toward a denial of emotional pain must play a role in the heavy emphasis that is placed upon the *physical* aspects of violence toward children. Most would define 'abuse' toward children as involving only physical injury.

As a society, we do not, as yet, recognize the emotional impact (or trauma) that can occur as a result of spanking, hitting, swatting, popping, tapping, or patting (or whatever other euphemism might be used to describe inflicting a degree of violence upon children). We generally don't conceive of the possibility that a perfectly 'legal' spanking can involve an emotionally abusive beating. We simply tend to deny this possibility, as evidenced by the fact that we all know children experiencing their first taste of violent behavior from a parent seldom begin to scream in agony as the result of the physical pain that's being inflicted on them. We might even hear a parent exclaim, 'Shut up, or I'll *really* give you something to cry about!'

The screaming that many of us have heard coming from a young child being struck is not so much the result of physical trauma as it is emotional trauma. The overwhelming emotional pain of rejection, worthlessness, and the betrayal of trust is usually much more potentially damaging than the force of the blows.

Where we adults are concerned, being subjected to this kind of distress has been termed 'Emotional Pain and Suffering' and our legal system will often award us compensation for such a violation of our personal well-being and emotional stability. Yet, although the potential for long term emotional damage is much greater for children being treated in a violent manner than it is for us, we still choose to ignore, or deny, the emotional suffering of children related to legalized spankings (or other demeaning treatments).

Some parents try to convince themselves that if they offer hugs, and profess their love after engaging in the ultimate act of rejection toward their children, that this ritual will somehow negate the trauma, and potential emotional damage, they had just moments before inflicted upon their child. This thinking is similar to the wife-beater who, after victimizing his wife, tenderly professes his deep love for her in the belief that his offerings of love will compensate for the emotional damage he has caused her, as well as repairing any damage he may have caused to the quality of the relationship they share.

We've come to know full well that this hate-love ritual by violent husbands doesn't work on wives, and I'd like to suggest that neither does it work on children. Not only is the 'I hate you, now I love you' routine of spanking ineffective, it's a practice that can lead children to begin associating love with pain and violence.

Most people will be quick to recognize that bruises left on a child who has been spanked represents child abuse simply because that is the way the legal system currently defines 'abuse' as it relates to children under 18 years of age. What we, as a society, fail to consider is the possibility that while the bruises of abuse will soon heal, the emotional wounds of diminished self-esteem, anger, alienation, or depression, that are known to result from children being victimized by violent treatment, can remain open sores for a lifetime... regardless of whether or not physical injury occurred as a result of the violence.

If there are parents who are willing to claim that spanking their children has not, or will not, cause their children emotional harm, they must also be willing to make the claim that they themselves, would not be emotionally harmed by being treated in the same manner by their spouses or other loved ones. We simply can't afford to turn a blind eye to the undeniable reality that children suffer the same fear, dread, and alienation through being physically punished, as us adults. If we experience an unhealthy fear toward the prospect of being victimized by force and violence, it is nothing more than an act of humanity to consider that children suffer the same fear, to the same degree, as would we ourselves.

Sadly, according to the attitudes of some, one would imagine that children represent some different form of life that is somehow immune to the same feelings and emotions experienced by actual 'real' people. Fact is, we are all members of the same species who all share in common the same basic emotions. And in the same light, we also all share together a remarkably similar response to being treated in a violent manner (or threatened with such)... and our response involves a powerful compunction to either fight or run; we might hide if able, or we might shut-down emotionally (dissociate) in the event we find ourselves unable to either fight or run as a normal response (the fight or flight autonomic response to threat). Children often dissociate as their only defensive option given their circumstances.

We should remain mindful that the emotional beatings we suffer, both adult and child alike, as the result of being treated in violent ways, can leave us feeling diminished, insecure, debilitated, fearful, and emotionally unstable... maybe we suffer for a day, a week, or perhaps a month. But, then again, we might find ourselves struggling through emotional difficulties for years beyond the time when any physical wounds would have long since healed and been put far behind us.

EMOTIONAL HEARTBREAK

As I've said, many of us have known parents who, after hitting their child will say in response to the screams, 'Shut up, or I'll give you something to *really* cry about!' Regardless, I think most parents do realize that the child is not screaming as a result of the mere physical pain caused by being hit. As a matter of fact, most of us have probably witnessed a young child screaming over being struck on a well-padded bottom where it was unlikely that any physical pain was experienced at all.

It's a strange act of humanity when we strike a child and do so because 'It's just something you do to kids'. Why? 'Well, just because'. Some parents steel their hearts against these woeful wails of emotional suffering, and simply ignore the child, while others yet will become angry over all the noise being made by the cries. *Easy to Be Hard* went the lyrics of a song from the musical, *Aquarius*... and as a famous basketball commentator would say, 'No harm, no foul!'

Parents can offer plenty of excuses for hitting their kids, but cannot offer any sound reasons for doing so. One can observe this type of response from parenting board to parenting board across the Internet. Many of these parents ask, 'Why is spanking abusive when no physical injury is inflicted?' The thinking seems to be that if the wound cannot be seen, it just never happened. Some parents have become so immune to the emotional suffering of children that when they are told that hitting a child can break the bond of trust between the parent and the child, they say 'I don't get it'. Or, when they are told that this heartbreak on the part of the child also involves a sense of betrayal, they say 'What are you talking about?', and when they are told that the screams of pain involve feelings of rejection and worthlessness, they say 'huh?' yet again.

We really can't make the claim that 'inhuman human behavior' is an oxymoron, can we? Is this kind of behavior toward those we love just a part of who we are, or does it represent a sickness of the human spirit? My vote is for the latter. It's a sickness of irrational proportions afflicting those who possess the capability to treat children in such a manner.

As adults, we can easily see how having our hearts broken time after time will cause us to become leery about the notion of love. We can understand that if someone were being hit and demeaned by the only person in the world that they had to depend on, then the victim might become highly distraught, fearful, and insecure. We can also understand that if we get emotionally hurt time and again in relationships, we tend to withdraw socially; we'll lose confidence in ourselves; and we might develop a fear of commitment and begin relating to others on a strictly superficial level. For some reason, it is not as easy for us to see that the same possible consequences of being emotionally hurt might hold true for children as well.

Some of the heartbreak I've experienced has come through parents thinking that they can tell their kids they love them while behaving in a manner toward them that conveys rejection, and then deluding themselves into believing that paying lip service to love will carry the day. If purposefully inflicting pain upon a child (or upon anyone, for that matter) is not the ultimate act of rejection and loathing, then I don't know what is. Haven't we all seen the expression on a parent's face as they raise a hand to strike their child? Is there a time when we humans can look more hateful, fearsome, brutal, and just plain ugly? Doesn't there have to be something wrong with this picture when these same people normally strive to be just as gentle and kind as they can be when dealing with the rest of humanity?

Too many of us have ignored a child crying out in emotional pain and anguish. If we can ignore that, well... it wouldn't be much of a stretch to guess that we're capable of steeling ourselves against the pain of other human suffering as well.

SPANKING AS A PREJUDICE AGAINST CHILDREN

To further clarify my previous remarks, I'd like to discuss the practice of spanking children as it relates to acts of physical aggression against women and minorities. It shouldn't be seen as unreasonable to address the act of spanking as a practice that represents an attitudinal behavior that is highly indicative of a discriminatory prejudice against children... no differently than is the case for other members of our society.

It's been said that kids benefit from a good spanking. Some people justify this practice by claiming that today's kids are getting out of control, and need to be punished more severely. These same people might be surprised to learn that this generational view has been expressed toward a number of specific social groups throughout our history.

When I hear these prejudicial generalizations, I'm reminded of the sexist fellow I once overheard complaining to his buddy about how today's women were getting so high and mighty that if you made them angry or didn't give them their way, you just might wake up in the morning minus an important body part. We all recognize such statements against women as prejudiced, but I find it somewhat curious that the same types of statements made against children are not generally perceived as prejudiced at all. Such statements made against children generally seem perfectly acceptable on a social level.

Indeed, it would seem that as a society, we don't recognize negative stereotypes applied to children as being prejudiced, bigoted, or discriminatory. Unlike any other distinguishable segments of our population, regardless of race, religion, gender, or ethnic background, we see that children alone are the only societal group within our population that remains fair-game for stereotypical ridicule, double standards of treatment, and discriminatory regard. Perhaps most notable is the fact that children are the only segment of our society still remaining unprotected by the umbrella of laws governing crimes of assault. These are the laws that protect every adult member of our society from the practice of routine corporal punishments, including our most violent imprisoned criminals.

On a societal level, the crux of the spanking issue centers on a prejudicial view that continues to allow children to remain as the last members of the human race who are still not considered as the type of human beings that deserve the same level of legal protections from acts of violence as the rest of humanity. So, for the sake of this argument, it's not the practice of spanking, per se, that serves as the focal point of argument. Rather, I'll be addressing a motivating factor behind the practice of spanking that is seen in the form of a prejudicial attitude toward children that allows an adult to feel justified in raising a hand to a child for punishment to begin with. In this particular case of stereotypical group prejudice, the existence of the prejudice is evidenced by the great preponderance of those who express a willingness to strike children while at the same time expressing an unwillingness to strike any other misbehaving members of society, not even for the same reasons used to justify hitting children.

In the classic work of literature within the study of human behavior, *The Authoritarian Personality* (Adorno, et al.), it was concluded that the personality type most given to negative stereotypes, prejudices, bigotry, and discriminatory behavior could be categorized as the 'Authoritarian Personality Syndrome'. There is probably nothing that bears-out these findings more clearly than the problematic consequences we see in the authoritarian nature of parental attitudes toward children.

It is the authoritarian approach toward child rearing which stands alone as the causal factor in children being held to a prejudicial lower standard of treatment. It's a standard that is most represented by a fixed belief that children need (and implicitly deserve) to be kept under control through the establishment of fear and intimidation on the part of parents (and other authority figures).

This form of parent-child relationship is invariably associated with punitive acts of physical aggression being initiated by parents against their children as an acceptable practice. As we know, these acts involving varying degrees of violence being inflicted upon children are euphemistically referred to as spankings. Not surprisingly, establishing parental dominance through the use of overpowering physical force for the purpose of causing physical pain and humiliation has traditionally served as the preferred method of punishment for children. This parenting practice has been long recognized by parents as the quickest, most effective and convenient means by which to control the behavior of children... with fear and intimidation serving as secondary motivating factors.

It's my view that a more strenuous effort should be made to take the wheels out from under the well-oiled steamroller of authoritarian parenting. Spanking is the hub in the wheel of authoritarian attitudes toward child rearing. If the hub can be discarded as unacceptable, the authoritarian wheel will irreparably collapse in favor of yet another step toward a greater humanity.

Many parents who spank seem to be under the impression that the only noteworthy risk carried by this violent form of punishment involves the possibility of causing a small degree of physical harm, such as bruises or welts. It is extremely rare to find a spanking parent who is willing to address, or recognize, the existence of harmful emotional consequences related to spanking. Yet, the truth of the matter is that it's the *emotional* consequences of the spanking environment that pose the greatest long term risk to the well-being of children.

As a motivating force and precursor to whatever outcomes might result from spankings, there can be little doubt that the greatest threat posed to the healthy emotional growth and development of children is found in the ageist, authoritarian attitude toward children. It's this preju-dicial attitude that allows for the degree of disrespect necessary to jus-tify a willingness to hit children in the first place. And, it's an attitude that's as old as time. It reflects the same disrespect that was once seen being displayed toward other so-called 'lesser' or 'undeserving members' of our society. These were other offending groups of people who were usually unwelcome on the basis of their race, religion, ethnic background, gender, or sexual preference.

Historically, these groups of people have been those members of society who, along with children, also found themselves labeled as just one more group of second class citizens to be viewed with such preju-dicial disrespect by the white Christian majority that they made suitable candidates to become the victims of violent crimes of hate.

It shouldn't come as a shock to learn that these crimes of hate against minority groups happen to represent acts of physical aggres-sion born of the same prejudicial attitudes that serve as the basis for hitting children. At various past points in time, children shared their level of social-status with others viewed in lowly regard and question-able worth. Aside from children, these other second-class citizens of our society have included Native Americans, African Americans, women, homosexuals, alcoholics, unwed mothers, witches, sorcerers, atheists/heathens, bastard children, prostitutes, bums/hobos/homeless, ex-convicts, drug fiends, any immigrant group, and foreigners. I don't believe that there was a single immigration group to come into the US that escaped being subjected to an initial period of being treated as inferior second-class citizens.

Prejudice is one of our more ugly, harmful, and dangerous human shortcomings. We've now grown beyond all but one socially accepted group prejudice in terms of physical punishments. Wouldn't it be nice to

96 The Road to Positive Discipline

scrape-off the last ugly remnants of prejudice from the bottoms of our shoes and put a final end to acceptable social injustice?

One exceptionally germane example of this group prejudice I've been referring to is the one well known by the female segment of our society. It's been popularly described as misogyny, male chauvinism, or more recently, sexism. Most women are familiar with the prejudiced attitude this kind of knuckle-dragging, sexist man holds toward women. True enough, he can often justify hitting a woman. These individuals display an element of contempt that seems to accompany a generalized view of man's innate superiority over the so-called weaker sex. It's a discriminatory attitude that allows this type of man to convey a degree of disrespect that sometimes justifies the use of physical force as a means of imposing his will upon his woman (perhaps even a good occasional spanking to remind her of who it is that's boss of the household).

If any spanking parents happen to find the above scenario barbaric, brutish, and wholly despicable, please hold that thought as I point out the fact that the prejudicial attitude of the misogynist is the same exact prejudicial attitude that allows parents to treat their children in the same manner.

To help illustrate my point, let me ask the women readers what they would find as the most upsetting thing about being in a relationship that included being non-injuriously spanked as a punitive measure. To simplify matters, let's suppose that the dearly beloved man, in whose trusted hands you had placed the whole of your care, safety, and well-being, began to discipline you with spankings. And, this occurs while living under conditions that render it impossible for you to escape from the relationship at any time in the foreseeable future. You are totally dependent on this man for your survival and are completely powerless to effect any change in the existing circumstances.

If you can imagine how you would feel and react to these kinds of living conditions, you have taken the first step in being able to empathize with the feelings that spanked children find themselves facing in the home. Of course, it goes without saying that you are much better emotionally equipped than a young child to successfully cope with such conditions.

In the hope that there are some spanking moms who would be interested in perhaps gaining a better understanding of why children do what they do, and feel what they feel, I'd like to offer the following questions for your consideration.

In the above outlined scenario, do you think that you would consider the acts of being spanked against your will as the most emotionally disturbing element in your relationship with your dearly beloved husband? Or, rather than the act itself, would it be what the act represents in terms of conveying the message that you are regarded as an inferior being that is deserving of being controlled through violent measures? Would it not mean to say that you are seen as less adequate, less competent, less intelligent, deserving of being stripped of your dignity, and unworthy of the respect this man is willing to give others, but not you? Can you think of anything that he could do that would be more distressful, or more threatening to your continued sense of well-being than finding yourself being coerced by a needed loved one each time he thought you failed him as a person, with each blow serving as a reflection of your inability to live-up to his expectations?

In addition, just as this prejudice works against children, his willingness to control you through physical force and pain reflects a disrespectful attitude toward women that would also leave you highly subject to related forms of expressed prejudice, such as finding yourself being made the target of demeaning humor in front of his friends or in public.

Perhaps some of you may have been able to imagine yourselves living under the abusive conditions I've outlined above. Might it seem that this prejudiced, authoritarian attitude being directed toward you might be more emotionally damaging and cause a greater degree of harm to the relationship than the actual occurrences of being the victim of physical aggression? After being intimidated, forcefully overpowered, and compromised, do you think that the number of blows landed upon you as punishment would have any significant bearing upon the extent of personal diminishment you'd be experiencing? If so, might this feeling of personal diminishment also cause you to experience a decrease in the level of your self-esteem and personal worth? Well, regardless of how any answers might differ, it is nevertheless true that no one thrives in such a prejudicial environment, neither man, woman, nor child.

Regardless of age, *all* victims of prejudice suffer in mind, body, and spirit... physical harm or not.

Spanking In Love?

How violence may have become an act of love.

Time and again, some (usually conservative Christians) exclaim that spanking their children is an 'act of love', with the violence being inflicted upon the children 'with love'. The notion holds that a child can be hit in a positive, respectful, and loving manner. It may be a good excuse for spanking, but from where would such a contradictory, illogical concept originate? It would seem that children are the only segment of humanity who can be 'loved' while being abused (with the possible exception of wife-beaters who will also at times claim that hitting their woman is done 'in love', and 'because of love', and 'for the sake of love'). Well, I have a thought on how this convoluted definition of 'loving behavior' may have come about as it relates to the brand of violent Christian parenting that still persists to this day throughout the world.

At some point in time, there may have been an evangelical member of the clergy who was attempting to reconcile the teachings of Jesus Christ with the teachings of King Solomon. With Christ promoting the concepts of love, compassion and forgiveness, it's understandable that this cleric would have had great difficulty trying to figure out how he could justify telling his flock that their inherently evil children needed to have the devil beat out of them. With Christ saying things like, 'however you would treat your lessers is how you would treat me', and, 'love your enemies as you would love yourself', as well as, 'do unto others as you would have them do unto you', how could this cleric justify sermonizing to his congregation that children should be beaten with a rod or they would be hated by their parents, as taught by Solomon in the Old Testament Book of Proverbs?

Perhaps he came to the decision to simply promote the idea that acts of violence committed against children were actually acts of 'loving' behavior. By introducing an expanded definition of love to include violence toward children, parents would be able to strike their kids with impunity as merely another expression of their love for Him. If this leader of the church were asked by his flock how love could be expressed through violence, he would simply tell them that God works in mysterious ways.

And so it came to pass that parents began hitting their children as an expression of their love for them, and we have come to hear things said to children like, 'I'm only hitting you because I love you'.

Certainly, the above scenario is speculation on my part (after all, it may have been a whole council of church elders who came up with the concept of 'violence as loving behavior'). But nevertheless, it seems apparent that the last societal institution standing as a bastion of support for violence toward children lies in the teachings of conservative Christianity.

With dogma stating that children need to be purged of their evil ways and sinful natures through loving violence, the excuses to perpetuate the practice of spanking children would seem compelling to the great majority of blindly devout followers of this particular religious orientation.

Sadly, this violence toward children, coupled with expressions of love and affection, is most certainly a major (if not exclusive) cause of children developing an association between violence and loving behavior. This is an unnatural conditioning that comes through an unconscious attempt to fulfill their basic need for love. Unfortunately, this dysfunctional learning can lead children into later tolerances of abusive relationships, or leave them prone to the development of sado-masochistic proclivities.

I fully appreciate the fact that some people can be made to believe anything. But, if there are any die-hard spankers reading this who find themselves attracted to the idea of defining 'spanking' as an act love, please don't try to convince your kids of this thinking. Again, children possess a need for love so powerful that some of them will buy into just about any behavior a parent chooses to define as loving in nature... even acts of violence.

The negative consequences inherent in teaching kids that an act of physical aggression is a part of loving behavior represents both a terrible disservice to children as well as an egregious act of parental irresponsibility.

PRO-SPANKING ARGUMENTS

Following are most of the standard rationalized justifications that parents use as an excuse for spanking children. Sadly, as can be seen, the excuses lack merit.

1. 'I was spanked, yet I am not violent in any way!' The problem with this argument is that it simply denies reality. The statement should actually say, 'I was spanked as a child, and I am not violent in any way... except toward children, of course'. It is a rare occasion indeed to encounter a spanking parent who was not spanked as a child.

2. 'Spanking is not violence'. This is another position of simple denial on the part of parents. This denial may, in large part, result from their early-on orientation to violence toward children because being hit as a child became a part of their accepted reality. The child comes to learn that while violence in general is a bad thing, adults hitting children is perfectly acceptable, and cannot therefore fall under the definition of violence. This is another truism illustrated by the fact that striking another adult on the buttocks for the purpose of inflicting punitive pain is defined by society as an act of violence, whereas, striking a child in the same manner is defined as 'spanking', or 'discipline', and somehow different than the same act as it applies to adults.

3. 'We are violent by nature'. This is a misnomer. While we are born with the mechanisms that can trigger violent behavior (biologically designed as a survival mechanism for self-preservation through self-defense), we cannot correctly deem potential behaviorisms to be our nature any more than we can deem our potential to become psychotic as a part of our nature. The facts are contrary to this 'violence-oriented' position. We are born as social beings, and our nature is to love and be loved. These elements of our nature are so profound that an infant will not develop normally in the absence of love, and will not only fail to thrive, but will sometimes even fail to survive. Our true nature is demonstrated by our strong natural preference for peace and harmony over violence, hate, and discord.

4. 'There is no evidence to show that a little violence ever hurt anyone'. This is a rationalization that could also be expressed by saying that 'there is no evidence to show that just a little arsenic ever killed anyone'. It's a position that denies the *risk* factors involved with behavior... and where spanking is concerned, there are a number of risks that have been well established and documented.

5. 'Spanking is not a 'moral' issue'. On a societal and religious basis, this is another misnomer. It would be hard to argue that most of us have reached a point of social sophistication to where we would agree that finding non-violent solutions to problems and difficulties represents the moral high ground.

6. 'Other things can mess kids up too'. True enough. Such things as hanging-by-the-thumbs, verbal abuse, or failing to be provided adequate nutrition, can also have negative influences on the well-being of children. But as with spanking, none of these things are warranted, healthy, or advisable.

7. The argument holding that, 'pain is a good learning experience and we sometimes even seek it out for ourselves', is an invalid argument that should be self-explanatory. Pain, under normal circumstances, is obviously a biological warning sign of a threat to our well-being. I believe it's safe to conclude that something has gone awry with the normal scheme of things when this excuse is used as a justification for inflicting physical pain upon children as an acceptable method of control/punishment.

8. There is also a spanking mentality holding that 'the world is a jungle. You either eat or get eaten. Kids need to be prepared for these ugly, but inevitable eventualities of life, and a familiarization with violence, cruelty, and harsh discord serves as good preparation for this brutal world our children must one day face on their own'. The consequences of this mentality too often result in the perpetuation of these views toward others, society, and life in general... with fear and distrust serving as the primary element of social discourse.

9. 'Children must learn to 'respect authority''. Truth is, spanking teaches children to *fear* authority, not respect it. Additionally, as a life-lesson, spanking does not prepare children for an adulthood where they will be physically assaulted for disrespecting authority as a punishment because non-injurious spanking as a

punishment for adults constitutes the crime of assault and battery (with the use of an implement/weapon for the spanking becoming aggravated assault).

10. And perhaps the most common misnomer, 'Spanking is a good learning tool to use for teaching children'. Fact is, the brain processes all cognitive learning in the same manner. Learning theorists have shown that punitive measures are counterproductive within a learning environment. Children learn how to behave by the same process as they learn how to read; yet we already know better than to punish children for making repeated mistakes while they are learning in an academic setting.

I'll finish with one of the more convoluted, if not bizarre, euphemisms I've seen in defense of striking children.

11. 'Non-injurious degrees of violent physical aggression used against children can be justified because they represent nothing more than another form of tactile communication that can be inflicted with love'. This is a rather ominous argument because it lumps 'loving behavior' together with 'hateful behavior' as being beneficial, and perfectly acceptable. What's sad about this argument is that it shows how the violent treatment of children can cause them to not only develop an orientation to violence, but also cause them to confuse loving behavior with pain and violence. This argument could be used in an attempt to justify strangling someone by the throat through simply deeming the act to be just another form of tactile communication. I believe that much better euphemisms for hitting children would be 'hard touching', or 'forceful caresses', or perhaps even 'gentle violence'.

A few other arguments in favor of spanking may have been overlooked here, but if so, they are probably even less rational than those mentioned above.

THE DEBATE ON SPANKING IS DEAD

I feel it's important to make it very clearly known to any and all concerned, that the debate on spanking within the scientific and academic communities is dead, and has been for a number of years now. The most substantial indicator of this development is evidenced by the fact that virtually every professional organization in the U.S. and Canada concerned with the care and treatment of children, has taken a public stance against the practice of spanking.

Based on the overwhelming accumulation of research conducted over the past 50+ years linking spanking to a number of risk factors, the professional consensus against this practice has grown to worldwide proportions... even to the extent that Sweden, Finland, Austria, Norway, Croatia, Denmark, Hungary, Israel, Cyprus, Netherlands, Bulgaria, Germany, Latvia, Iceland, Romania, Greece, New Zealand, Venezuela, Spain, Portugal, Chile, Uruguay, and Ukraine have legislated total bans on spanking... with Italy, South Africa, Scotland, Canada, and Ireland apparently in the process of following suit. It should also be noted that every industrialized country in the world has banned spanking in schools. The evidence is in, and the evidence has found against the practice of spanking in a compellingly conclusive manner.

Just as one might find supportive views toward spanking being promoted (typically) on websites sponsored by fundamentalist Christian sects, so can one find supportive views promoting homophobia, racism, misogyny, and other 'hate group' propaganda. Because of the fact that the actual agendas of these sites are often deceptively disguised by organizational titles such as, 'Family Council', 'People's Choice', 'Rights and Freedoms', etc., people are forced to exercise a highly judicious discernment of the information being made available on the Internet. Some web surfers have had to learn the hard way that the Internet abounds with persuasive presentations of 'facts and figures' that can prove to represent nothing more than religious, political, or philosophical attempts to spread self-serving misinformation.

Having spent 30+ years examining/evaluating the research on this issue of spanking children, I am able to state with a high degree of confidence that there has never been a peer-reviewed study that has been able to establish the efficacy of spanking as a means of long term behavior modification; as an effective teaching modality; as an effective punishment; or as a means of instilling self-discipline. Nor have there been published research findings in peer-reviewed professional journals that served to refute previous research. This previous research found spanking to be associated with a risk for undesirable emotional consequences; a risk for physical injury; a risk of counter-productive behavioral outcomes; a risk for the onset of dependence on external controls; and a proclivity toward authority-directed behavior. Moreover, there has never been research data produced finding that spanking carries no risk to the quality of the parent-child relationship (and I should add that conservative editorial reviews of previous research findings do *not* constitute actual research, as is sometimes claimed to be the case).

Nevertheless, there are some spankers who will find reasons to dismiss, ignore, or discount, the research findings of field conducted experimental studies related to the Social Sciences. Well, it's especially these individuals that I'd like to address concerning recent alarming research findings, which represent the some of the most severe potential consequences of physical punishment yet discovered.

Brain research has found that normal brain development in infants and young children can be severely impacted in abusive, neglectful home environments. Common sense tells us that this does not eliminate the possibility of a lesser degree of brain damage occurring to spanked children who are subjected to a lesser degree of non-injurious violence or neglectful conditions. In other words, it would be ludicrous to assume that a child must first become the victim of broken bones or severe emotional trauma (or other injuries) before brain damage can occur. Rather, it is much more logical to deduce that acts of physical aggression toward young children can disrupt, or prevent, the optimal conditions necessary to facilitate a normal process of healthy brain development.

As far as I'm concerned, this relatively new area of research represents the most compelling, undeniable reason that's yet been discovered to persuade parents to stop (or never start) striking their children as a punitive measure. And I hope any pro-spankers reading this feel the same way. It's difficult to imagine any parent who would be willing to treat their child in a way that might carry even a remote risk of causing a measure of brain damage to their child.

But, in spite of having said all of that, we actually shouldn't need research to end the practice of striking children any more than we needed research to end the practice of striking wives. As a society, there was no need for research findings to convince us of the harmful effects associated with the practice of wives being physically punished.

Instead, when society reached the point of being no longer willing to grant social tolerance to the tradition of husbands physically disciplining their wives, our decision to do so was based on our having progressed socially into the higher morality of a greater humanity. Perhaps, our next step ahead in forward progress should come by way of reaching a decision to begin recognizing children as also being deserving of those same protections against being struck.

No longer do we see any adult members of our society remaining outside the jurisdiction of the protective laws once enjoyed by only the more privileged and 'deserving' (namely white males who made the laws), regardless of race, gender, religion, ethnic group, or sexual orientation. None of our adult citizens remain legally unprotected from being violated through harassment, threats, defamation, discrimination, or being victimized by violence to any degree or form. So, given our heritage of bestowing a greater humanity upon those of a lower social status by welcoming them as our equals in the eyes of the law (in terms of violent treatment), would it be so out of character for us to also shelter the younger, weaker members of our society by allowing them to join those of us already sharing in the security and comfort of safety that's provided under the umbrella of legal protections from violence?

Bringing our little ones into the fold really doesn't seem all that magnanimous if we keep in mind that we've already been willing to share the shelter of our umbrella of assault laws with even the most vicious of hardened adult criminals. After all, children are the very last segment of our shared human collective who still remain as fair game for being subjected to acts of physical aggression. We display a strange sense of priorities when we don't allow the prison guard to break-out a paddle and start whacking away on the disobedient buttocks of a sociopathic death row inmate, yet we find helpless, defenseless young children as deserving of such treatment.

Fact is, we define corporal punishments of prison inmates as 'cruel and unusual punishment', 'guard brutality', or 'aggravated assault'. And, if the physical punishments should be repeated as a routine punitive measure, such a treatment of prisoners would fall under the definition of 'torture'.

Why would a murderous inmate be less subject to physical discipline than a helpless 3-year-old child?

Logically, morally, humanely, and scientifically, the debate on spanking is dead... save for those who would object to further social progress.

As we continue to evolve as a society, we have to keep in mind that historically there was a time when it was acceptable to legally own other people; a time when the mentally ill were generally considered to be possessed by evil spirits; a time when men legally shot each other in officiated duels; a time when public hangings were attended as a family outing complete with picnic basket; a time when public floggings were considered acceptable punishment; a time when it was a gentleman's agreement that husbands should not beat their wives with a switch that was 'bigger-round than your thumb' (which later became known as 'the rule of thumb'); and there was a time when there were no laws against parents severely beating their children (killing children was unacceptable, of course, but an occasional accidental maiming as a result of disciplinary measures was tolerated).

Obviously, we no longer permit these punishments. The time has come for us to yet further our level of social sophistication by coming to a general agreement that any degree of physical punishment used against children is as socially unacceptable and repugnant as those past violent behaviors we have chosen to put behind us.

SOCIAL ISSUES

CRIMINAL TREATMENT

I would like to suggest that a discussion of our attitudes toward criminal behavior is most germane to a discussion of how we discipline our children.

Clearly, our society (U.S.) is punitively oriented to a greater degree than most other developed countries (especially Western Europe). I would suggest that this orientation toward punishment is developed during the formative years of childhood in association with our child rearing practices.

Let me preface my remarks by discussing those unlawful behaviors that leave us with a desire to have our 'pound of flesh'. A lack of empathy is a primary characteristic of anti-social behavior, as well as sociopathy. Through my research and experience, I've determined that there is a clear link between low-level parenting skills (which include the practice of spanking) and deficiencies in the development of empathy in children. It's important to note that neglectful parenting practices often go hand-in-hand with authoritarian parenting practices.

I believe that the determining factor involved in these circumstances is the extent to which parents fail to meet the emotional needs of their children. Obviously, the practice of spanking children not only fails to satisfy their emotional needs, it's a practice that creates a deficiency in need fulfillment. This is one of the major risks associated with subjecting children to violent treatments of any degree... whether it be 'smacks' on the hand, 'pops', 'taps', 'swats', 'spankings', 'light occasional spankings', or any of the other euphemistic terms used to describe the violent treatment of children.

There are those who were spanked as children, but were nevertheless fortunate enough to develop strong empathetic abilities. I'd suggest that this transpires as the result of these children having received a sufficient amount of nurturing to enable them to overcome the parental counter-measures taken against the adequate fulfillment of their emotional needs. And, clearly, parents cannot compensate for their violence by striking their child while saying the words, 'I love you so much, my dear child'. The associative risk of violence toward children in these 'loving' circumstances is obvious, but it's nevertheless a risk often recklessly denied by spanking parents.

There is simply no parent in this world who can say with reliable confidence that their capacity for love, and their nurturing abilities, will adequately compensate for the degree of negative emotional impact carried by their acts of violence taken against their children. It should be a given that violence against another serves as the ultimate form of rejection. I should also note that we really don't appreciate how many children failed by parents are emotionally saved by relatives and other caretakers who provide desperately needed nurture.

I don't relate well to the general concept of 'rehabilitation' as it relates to our penal system because the word seems to be too often associated with merely throwing someone in a cage to 'straighten him or her out by giving them time to think about what they've done'. Instead, I prefer to approach this concept in terms of how we can best address the problem of anti-social behavior through treating the emotional damage that lies behind this form of behavior.

As I've said, we are born into this world as social beings by nature. Although some mistakenly believe otherwise, we are not born with a propensity to cause harm to others. Rather, a desire to harm others is actually contrary to our nature. This is evidenced by the fact that our social nature includes a powerful basic drive for love and acceptance, which serves as the basis for our emotional needs. With this in mind, it's not difficult to surmise that the great majority of behavioral problems in children, most notably of an anti-social nature, occur as the result of unmet emotional need.

The question we need to ask ourselves is to what extent can we successfully treat the emotional damage that has caused the victim to become the agent of subsequent victims?

Would it be fair to speculate that murderers are untreatable based on our tendency to forgo any meaningful treatment modality? Of course, we don't know the answer to this because we've lacked the will to pursue alternative long term treatment modalities that could prove effective. Rather, we've always been of a mind to instead keep them locked-up or put to death.

So, as things stand now, there are those who suffer irreparable emotional damage during the formative years that becomes manifested in anti-social behavior. Consequently, violent criminals will need to be kept segregated from mainstream society for safety sake. I'm not going to argue that fact. But, what of all those lesser offenders who have committed anti-social acts based on an upbringing that has left them filled with the anger and rage of unmet emotional need? They serve their time, pay their debt to society, and get paroled. Do they come back out into the world only able to assume that they are going to be facing the same harsh emotional deprivations as a part of the only real-ity they have ever known? It would be hard to deny this possibility. So, how should we best treat someone who views society with hostility, guarded distrust, alienation, and contempt? If the world is viewed as a cruel and uncaring place that will not hesitate to cause hurt and pain, why would such persons care if they did some hurting right back as a means of retribution?

Well, we're apparently a society that is not quite ready to consider questions such as those, so what it is we do is fulfill the expectations of these hostility-ridden individuals by treating their past hurts with more hurt, such as demoting their social-status to that of second-class citizen in terms of rights, privileges, and job opportunities. Moreover, we actu-ally believe this to be the most effective method of treatment. What we actually do is simply feed the anger and alienation. Granted, our cul-tural values demand that these people be held accountable for their behavior and punished so that they can be 'taught a lesson', however counter-productive that lesson may be. But, would it prove constructive if we were to at the same time reach-out to these offenders with a car-ing hand of help and concern instead of pushing them further away with a rejecting, disapproving cold fist of harsh regard? Is it really wise for us to imprison socially alienated offenders in an environment designed to further alienate them? By offering assistance, would it be sensible to assume that this could serve to alleviate the level of anti-social tenden-cies in those who have never known what it was to get a fair shake in life?

While it is true we continue to move further in this direction by of-fering prisoners educational programs, group therapy sessions, etc., the assistance we offer appears to convey more begrudging reluctance than caring concern. The predominant thinking still seems to hold that offenders should not be coddled with caring regard for a rehabilitative process. Rather, we banish these considered 'low-life' criminals from society by locking them in a cage and proceeding to strip them of their human dignity... even in the case of victimless crimes. We're obviously more interested in exacting retribution and vengeance upon wrong-doers than we are in rehabilitation, or even restitution being made to victims of less serious offenses.

Anti-social behavior *is* treatable in many cases and until we recog-nize this behavior as a mental disorder precipitated by emotional dam-age, we will continue to punish such behavior as a personally and socially counter-productive method of treatment. I confirmed this notion of 'anti-social behavior as responsive to treatment' for myself as a re-sult of spending three months interviewing maximum security prisoners as a part of my research for a paper on the emotional effects of imposed isolation. The consequences are invariably negative, and render the individual a greater threat to society than they had been previously.

THE EVOLUTION OF A GREATER HUMANITY

Since the start of this new millennium, we have even more talk about how 'the end is drawing near', about the 'decline of society', and we ironically hear more about how we need to increase the severity of punitive measures for children in order to stem the tide of the out-of-control level of violence we see in the world today. I'd like to offer a counter-point to the position that we are de-evolving into a less humane species.

My interest in the topic of 'man's inhumanity to man' began in 1968 while taking a course in Western Civilization. I remember being struck by the fact that the audiences of Ancient Greece (the world's model for Democracy) used to stone (sometimes to death) the actors in theater productions who were seen as not meeting acceptable performance standards. It was disappointing for me to also learn that this civilization, which is often held in tribute as having given birth to the democratic process, was also a country of city-states that were perpetually at war with one another. This supposedly sophisticated society wasn't really all that sophisticated after all!

I started thinking that perhaps mankind is not as violent, cruel, or brutal as it once was. I began to see more examples of how this might be true. Then, as the years passed, I came to learn that the evidence is indisputable... we are a species who continually evolves into more sophisticated behavior in terms of a greater humanity. We are beings whose propensity toward violence and brutality diminishes with each passing generation. Without question, we have over time, become generally more kind and gentle toward one another. If we start from the beginning of known history, specific examples of this historical fact are innumerable... and unquestionable.

Let me cite just a few of the more notable examples of our continual evolvement on a behavioral basis. The inhuman institution of legalized slavery has disappeared throughout the world compared to just a few centuries ago. The conquering and subjugation of weaker nations is no longer tolerated by the world community to the extent it once was. As a matter of fact, just seventy years ago, the world allowed an unjustified Germany to militarily roll right over the countries of Europe with only England and France declaring war against them at the start of the aggression. Today, the world community does not tolerate such blatant aggression against sovereign countries. Generally, the world as a whole views such conduct by a country as atrocious and intolerable (although action may not be taken for various political reasons).

From the beginning of recorded history, women have been beaten by their men as an acceptable form of punishment. We can track the allowable treatments of women from a time when adulterous wives were stoned to death to a time when the 'gentlemanly' thing to do was to not beat the wife with a switch 'bigger round than a thumb' (the rule of thumb), all the way to the present when those same Judeo-Christian societies have come to view the hitting of wives by any means, to be a criminal act. These changes in our behavior reflect social progress... they are also reflective of human behavior on an evolutionary scale.

We can look more specifically at our ever-increasing levels of behavioral sophistication by simply looking at the relatively recent changes in behavior reflected by the values and morés of American society. Just a couple of hundred years ago in the U.S., men of social stature were generally considered cowards if they failed to challenge another man to a shooting duel as a result of insulting remarks. As I've stated previously, gentlemen legally shot one another over personal disagreements and public hangings were viewed as a family affair. Children were maimed and sometimes beaten to death by parents who suffered no legal recourse. There were no cases of child abuse brought before the courts until the 1870's (the 'Mary Ellen Case').

Increases in our levels of greater humanity and continued growth can also be seen in much more subtle forms. Movies have certainly portrayed our societal evolution. Films that were made in our recent history where the 'leading man' and 'hero' of the movie, who was meant to portray the male model of manly behavior, could be seen giving a good spanking to an 'uppity' wife (John Wayne and Maureen O'Hara in *McLintock!* from 1963). Or, we could go back further in movie history to see a real man's man in the form of James Cagney squashing a grapefruit into the face of his disagreeing mistress (*The Public Enemy* in 1931). There are many other cinematic examples. These past behaviors unintentionally engendered responses from male audiences such as, 'Man, he showed her, didn't he? What a guy!' In the past, Hollywood male role models have played a role in the establishment of our cultural values.

We do not see such portrayals being made today. Currently, we all see how women are being cast in roles that show strength, courage, and capability. For example, Sigourney Weaver has fought, and defeated, a number of formidable aliens. Uma Thurman proved herself against all adversaries in *Kill Bill!*. There can be no doubt that movies represent a reflection of our societal evolvement.

We have seen the implementation of civil rights, equal rights, human rights, and even animal rights in our recent history. The ever-growing list of evidence of our social evolution into beings of a greater humanity continues to mount.

THE DOUBLE STANDARD OF ABUSE

When it comes to the crime of abuse, as it's defined on a legal and social basis, we hold animals and children to a lower standard of treatment. I don't mean that in a facetious way. The legal statutes designed to protect animals from physically abusive treatment are quite similar to those designed to protect children. As a matter of fact, animals enjoy a greater degree of protection than children in the sense that offenders can be charged with animal cruelty without necessarily causing observable marks (injuries) as a result of the physical punishment in question. We should take no pride in the fact that when we consider the perpetration of child abuse, as it's currently defined on a legal and social basis, we hold children to a comparable standard of treatment in relationship to the level of standards set for domesticated animals.

As most of us are aware, the laws protecting children are generally meant to protect them from physical injury related to disciplinary measures. It's interesting to note that until the early 1920's, women in the United States were offered no better degree of legal protection from spousal physical injury than the animals and children of today. In other words, until that time, women were also viewed by the men of society as being sufficiently inferior to be seen as needing, and deserving, the same corporal punishments as were being administered to children and animals.

As a society, we have a long history of holding children in low regard. The following account serves as a telling illustration of our traditional lack of regard for children. In New York City, during the 1870's, the courts agreed to hear the first case of child abuse in the U.S. It concerned the case of a young girl who had been severely battered and left abandoned to wander the streets of New York City. Because of the widespread publicity that ensued as a result of newspaper coverage, a legal course of action became politically judicious.

What transpired shocked the consciousness of many Americans because as the case unfolded, the public came to learn that the American Society for the Prevention of Cruelty to Animals of New York was representing this abused little girl in court (the 'Mary Ellen Case'). The reason this occurred is because we, as a society, had formed organizations for the protection of animals before any organizations had been formed to protect children. Consequently, there did not exist any organized societal structures designed to speak on behalf of the future welfare of this child in a court of law. Further evidence of this lack of societal regard for children can be seen in the fact that animal protection groups were approved as tax deductible charitable contributions *before* the same status was granted to children's protection groups.

From these beginnings, we still see to this day that our legal system considers it much easier to abuse an adult than it is to abuse a child. This is where the problems start with attempts to define 'abusive treatment' on a human level. It seems grossly unfair to hold another segment of humanity to a lesser standard of 'abuse' than we have set for ourselves... yet, that is precisely what we do when we apply more encompassing, self-serving definitions of 'abuse' to ourselves than we do to our children.

In the United States (and throughout the whole of Western Culture) it is unlawful to administer corporal punishment to *any* adult, under *any* circumstances. There are a number of designations that we have assigned to these acts as they apply to individuals over the age of eighteen. Incidents of corporal punishments perpetrated against adult victims are legally defined as assault and battery, aggravated assault, spousal abuse, and/or, domestic violence. The practice of corporal punishment within an institutional setting is defined as cruel and unusual punishment, and in some cases torture.

When it comes to children, however, the term 'lawful corporal punishment' becomes an altogether different matter. The basis for most of the confusion surrounding these differences in legal protections, treatments, and definition of terms can be attributed to the existence of the double standards that are applied to children. One of the more blatant examples of a double standard practiced against children can be seen through children being excluded from the right to be equally protected under the same umbrella of laws that protect adults from corporal punishments.

Unlike the broadly encompassing standards we employ to define the conditions under which we can feel justified in describing ourselves as having been a victim of abuse, children find themselves in a position where they are relatively unprotected from acts of assault. As things stand, the legal system makes it extremely difficult to prosecute a parent for child abuse without actual physical injury to the child having been observed by a credible third party, and then substantiated through an exhaustive investigative process.

Consequently, the generally held definition of child abuse involves physical injury to the child as the basic criteria characterizing this offense. Again, in contrast, we know full well that adults can qualify as victims of abusive treatment under much less severe circumstances than children. For example, we can see adults feeling wholly justified in describing themselves as having been cruelly abused by the mere confrontational, insulting *words* of another.

To clarify, let me put this issue in another way. I'm sure it wouldn't be difficult for anyone reading this to define as abusive a relationship where an overbearing, overly possessive, bully of a husband was treating his wife like an indentured servant. And, I think it would probably be safe to say that most people would describe this woman as being involved in an abusive relationship regardless of whether her husband had ever raised a hand to her. Here's the question. Is it just as easy to say that a child living under the same conditions as this woman is also being treated abusively? If not, why? Do we consider full-grown women to be more susceptible to emotional harm than young children, and therefore, more easily abused? Obviously, that is not true.

All things being equal, why would only one victim be given 'victim' status, with full legal recourse? It's been said that this is a moot question because the relationships between parent-child and husband-wife are different. But, that 'difference' is based on nothing more than a belief holding that an adult should be treated better than a child... as if adults had some magical right to be regarded with more kindness and respect than 'mere' children.

We also know that spouses who strike their mates in any manner whatsoever, regardless of the degree of physical aggression they employ, are nevertheless people who we have come to view as being guilty of spousal abuse. Gender doesn't matter, and the abuse can come in the form of 'message-sending', or 'attention-getting', or 'non-injurious swats' to serve as a reminder that the offending behavior will not be tolerated. The abuse might even come in the form of a good whack for learning to stay under the speed limit... or perhaps a quick, painful little pop on the butt to make sure the dry cleaning doesn't get forgotten the next time... heck, if there are those who have a bent for striking other human beings, they would probably have more reasons to hit their spouses than they would to hit their kids. Unfortunately, hitting our children is no less foolhardy than adopting the practice of hitting our spouses.

It would seem reasonable to conclude that this greater susceptibility to abuse on the part of adults indicates that we view children as being more physically resistant and emotionally stronger than us more seemingly fragile adults, who need the protection of the law. It's easy to see how the term 'abuse' can become confused depending on the age of the victim in question. Adding to this double standard conundrum is the fact that adults can be considered emotionally abused if verbally addressed in a rude, disrespectful manner. As we know, children are not given such consideration. For children, the crime of emotional abuse is practically non-existent, as it requires a much greater degree of substantiated evidence (with prosecutors often requiring a professional diagnosis of emotional impairment to the child). It could even be said that the very existence of these double standards that we impose upon our children are, in themselves, abusive in nature.

So, it appears that we adults consider children to be less susceptible to physical injury, spiritual diminishment, and emotional harm. Currently, it would appear that children are better able to cope with being physically and emotionally accosted than full-grown adults. As such, adults will continue to consider themselves assaulted and abused whenever they are struck by anyone who might feel it necessary to deliver them a punitive blow, whether physical or verbal.

THE FARCE OF 'INHERENT EVIL'

There can be no doubt in anyone's mind that one of the more egregious rationalized excuses for the practice of spanking lies in a belief that holds children liable for being born into this world with evil and sin in their hearts. Certainly, there are other ugly views of children as being 'part enemy' that can be attributed to this religious doctrine... such as views holding children to be little more than selfish, manipulative, dirty, rebellious, and wild little beings who need to be broken into submission, and forced into the ways of civilized humanity.

When looking at the history of our species, one of the more prevalent values held by past societies was a belief that the gods heaped natural disasters and hardships upon humanity as a punishment for misdeeds. Many past civilizations practiced human sacrifice as a means of appeasing the gods for the sins of Man.

At a time when there existed no understanding of why anyone would refuse to conform to the behavioral expectations and norms of society, the mystery of anti-social or other abnormal behaviors came to be explained away by the evil of supernatural forces, whose power lay beyond the control of humanity. In ancient societies, it was commonly held that the only way to treat those deemed to be under the control of these supernatural forces bent on destroying mankind was to execute them.

In Christianity, this demonological concept came in the form of one supernatural evil force (Satan), as a means to explain away otherwise inexplicable undesired behavior. As time went on, the Christian Church began to explore more humane treatments other than execution for those who were seen as being possessed or influenced by Satan. These new treatments came in the form of exorcism to chase out the demons spawned by the devil, or through using (originally) a sharp rock to pound a hole in the head of those who were seen as 'possessed' in an effort to allow the evil entity to escape from the mind of those so afflicted (the practice of this procedure was called 'trephining', and served as the first form of frontal lobotomy).

This demonological concept also holds that we are born into this world already influenced by this evil supernatural force known as the 'devil' or 'Satan'. It is a concept designed to serve as an explanation for our sinful ways by simply deeming humanity to be conceived under the influence of evil and, therefore, leaves us to be born with a desire to infest the world with sinful needs and evil intentions. While some denominations of Christianity have eschewed the dictum of 'born in sin', it apparently remains a doctrine still taught by a number of sects. As 'the work of the devil', this concept has served to explain away that which would otherwise remain inexplicable in terms of behavior which falls outside the parameters of behavior deemed acceptable by the church. While the inherent omnipresence of a lurking Satan serves as good justification for spiritual and financial devotion to the church, it has also become a concept serving to encourage and perpetuate the practice of spanking children.

After more than twelve years of observing adamant spanking proponents on a number of parenting websites, I have yet to see a pro-spanker who did not believe that children are born as despicable little urchins who are anxiously awaiting their first opportunity to make life miserable for parents. I've seen this attitude expressed toward children by mostly those who have been orientated to this view of children through religious training (the 'sinful nature' concept).

Ominous indeed, are the implications and risks associated with a belief holding that newborn infants are already infected and corrupted with an underlying desire to behave in sinful ways as a reflection of their evil nature. Parents holding this belief may pay lip service to the term 'unconditional love' but, just as they have been led to the conviction of 'inherent evil', it is just as likely that they have also come to be repulsed and frightened by this perception. It's only reasonable that the love of these parents becomes *highly* conditional when they see the underlying evil in their children finding an anxiously awaited opportunity to express itself. It is also reasonable to expect that these parents would want to fight, or eradicate, or destroy this horrid, demonic enemy of righteousness when it makes an appearance by way of their children. Violence would seem to be an expected reaction as a means to destroy or repulse the appearance of evil in the form of sinful behavior. We can see this reaction reflected in the originations of expressions such as 'beat the devil out of them', or 'knock the hell out of them', as a means to expel or destroy sinful behavior.

This type of parent also looks upon their newborn babies as possessing a flawed beauty, with ugly, sinful intentions lying just below the surface of a deceptively innocent demeanor. The relationship must involve a degree of distrust from the very beginning, with the parent needing to be constantly on guard against these sinful ways in children, which can erupt at any moment. With these sinful ways needing to be discouraged or purged as quickly as possible, it's no wonder that we can hear of parents striking their infants in the name of their god.

The study of human behavior has come a long way since the first attempts to explain unacceptable behavior. We've reached a point of accumulated knowledge and understanding regarding human behavior where it is much more reasonable and accurate to conclude that evil is *created* by humanity rather than humanity being born a servant to evil and sin by nature.

The Social Sciences have also come to recognize the crucial significance of self-esteem as a developmental characteristic necessary for children to behave in an emotionally healthy, fully functioning manner. Obviously, children being treated in a manner which reflects an attitude that they are naturally prone to sin, rather than being naturally prone to goodness, can in no way be considered a treatment which would be conducive to the development of healthy levels of self-esteem. Another problem with this concept is the 'Self-Fulfilling Prophecy'. This is an established psychological principle showing that children will behave in ways in which they are expected to behave. Children who are told they are born sinful and, consequently, come to view themselves as such, will tend to behave in sinful ways because they believe in what their parents have told them. This belief can become a part of the child's self-concept and actually determine *how* they behave because of who they see themselves to be.

I've come to the conclusion that the home environment creates 'evil' behavior. I have taken any existing empirical data in support of this notion a step farther. I've proven this conclusion by raising two children who were born in pure beauty and goodness, treated in beauty and goodness, and as a result, have grown to represent beauty and goodness. As adults, they now spread that same love, beauty, and goodness to those around them, and they have been rewarded by a world that seems very happy to have them around.

A child lost in the inadequacy of sin and badness is likely to develop a willingness to submit to a voice of authority and control through a feeling of being incompetent to function independently without strict guidance (external controls). But, a child basking in the glow of their perceived goodness is prepared to venture out into the world as an independent agent with a feeling they might be capable of making this world a better place in which to live through altruistic endeavor. No theory involved here... I've lived to see it for myself.

BASIC HUMAN RIGHTS FOR ALL

As a culture, we demand the basic human rights of freedom from violence, oppression, physical threat, and discrimination. Unfortunately, we somehow fail to include children as a part of humanity.

It seems apparent that many of us are seemingly imprinted with the notion that children should be treated in a less respectful manner than other human beings. Even some egalitarian and existential positions still fail to include children as a part of their philosophy.

Many of us find it extremely difficult to entertain the notion that children should be granted the same basic human rights that we demand for ourselves. This type of thinking predominates in spite of the fact that it would seem logical to grant children a greater leniency and tolerance with regard to their daily behavior. In light of the innocence of children, and their lack of understanding or knowledge as to how they should behave according to our culturally defined expectations, one would think that we would be less punitive toward children than we are toward ourselves on a daily basis. While they can be excused as novice students in the way of cultural expectations and the ways of the world, we adults, on the other hand, have no such justification for not following the rules of society.

It seems to me that if anyone is deserving of physical pain as a means of punishment, it should be us adults rather than children. After all, we should already know the rules of society, while children are still trying to learn what's expected of them. Of course, I am not suggesting that anyone should be subjected to physical pain. But, when we find ourselves forced to suffer punitive physical pain, we consider such treatment to be inhumane, cruel and unusual punishment, abusive treatment, and even torture in some cases. While many will support the idea of children being hit as a punitive measure, these are often the same people who will cry foul should they themselves ever be accosted for the same reasons.

Some people find it difficult to conceptualize a more esteemed view of our young. This prejudicial attitude stands as the major obstacle in the way of children becoming viewed as sufficiently worthy of being considered viable members of the human race along with the rest of us. Until we put such thinking behind us, it would seem fruitless to propose that we expand our definition of 'fairness' to include children under the umbrella of treatments we consider for ourselves to be fair, just, and humane.

I don't believe any of us would deny the wisdom and humanity offered by the Christian tenet, 'Do unto others as you would have them do unto you'. Most of us like that idea when it comes to interacting with other adults. But, we all pretty much know that when it comes to treating others as we ourselves would like to be treated, most of us exclude children as being 'people' or 'others'.

There was a time in our history when 'we the people' also excluded those brought to this country against their will, women, Native Americans, and immigrant groups, just as we see children being excluded today.

Well, times have certainly changed, and we can look with pride at the social progress we've achieved over the years in developing a greater degree of social sophistication. As evidence of this fact, we can point to the just fairness we've come to show toward minorities and women by affording them the same protections under the law, which had been previously enjoyed exclusively by white men.

It seems to me that if we are to remain on our path toward making continued strides in our social progress, a logical issue to now address should include one of our last remaining bastions of societal double standards, and discriminatory treatments... the lack of social-status granted to the children of our society. Of course, there are developmental issues concerning children that serve to limit their full participation in this adult world of ours, but that fact doesn't have a bearing on the unrelated circumstance involving equal protections under the law.

There is certainly no reason why we cannot at least begin to talk about granting children the same protection from violent treatment that we adults enjoy.

A note to spanking mothers

You want equality in your relationship with your husband, of course. You don't feel it would be acceptable for him to spank you for disobeying him or making repeated mistakes just because he is bigger and stronger than you are.

I totally agree with you. But, given this circumstance, I would like to ask, 'What makes you more susceptible to being abused than a child?' You can state that you don't deserve to be hit, but so would any child. That's not much of an argument. You can say that the relationship you have with your husband is 'different'. But, no loving relationship is 'different' when it comes to treating a loved one in a violent manner. You can say that you are 'responsible' for your kids as a justification for hitting them, just as I can take the position that a man is responsible for his wife and should, therefore, have the right to 'keep her in line'; to discourage her from embarrassing him in public; and to teach her to stop making the same mistakes all of the time. For every excuse you can state as a justification for hitting kids, I can counter with the same type of chauvinistic excuses for men hitting their wives as a means of discipline (as many husbands once did and, sadly, some still do).

The difference is that you are 'abused' if you get spanked against your will, while your children are not. I'm simply asking what it is that makes you think that you're better than a child, and therefore deserving of a more respectful treatment. Is it because you think that a spanking would be more harmful to you than it would be to a child?

Just as you moms would like to be legally protected from the threat of physical and emotional harm at the hand of a bullying husband, so should your children be protected in the same manner from the hand of a bullying parent.

A note to spanking fathers

Traditionally, it has been the males of society that have been most guilty of denying basic human rights to those viewed as smaller and weaker. We men have practiced the philosophy of 'might makes right' from the beginnings of known history. Perhaps we've come a long way from our knuckle dragging, cavemen ancestors. But men, it's time we evolved further beyond such atavistic tendencies. We've already evolved beyond corporal punishment as a routine means of controlling law-breakers and women. Let's take the next step up in our level of humanity by also putting behind us the corporal punishment of children as well.

We know from countless testimony (which young children are ill-equipped to provide) that all adults are emotionally harmed by threats or acts of violence to varying degrees, regardless of whether physical injury has occurred. The sad irony here is that young children are much more vulnerable to suffering emotional damage as the result of assaultive acts (including threats) than are we adults.

We should strive to grow beyond the inhumanity of socially accepted ageism in the same way that we've already progressed beyond the inhumanity of socially accepted racism and sexism. Given this, I support the notion that children should be afforded the same societal protections from violence as are enjoyed by the rest of society. After all, it's simply a position calling for basic human rights for *all* of us.

POSITIVE DISCIPLINE

WHY POSITIVE DISCIPLINE?

Because we have traditionally viewed children in a sub-standard light in terms of how they are regarded/treated, we have also come to change the way in which certain words are applied to them. 'Discipline' is one of those words. Over time, we have changed the definition of 'discipline', as it commonly applies to children, to mean 'punishment', or 'coercion'. Many of us fail to notice that the word 'discipline' is used differently when applied to adults.

To reiterate, the concept of discipline was originally intended to describe a 'learning-teaching' process, with the 'disciple' being the student. If we can look upon discipline related to parenting as a 'student-teacher' process, we can begin to see how the word 'positive' can be made a part of the term 'discipline'.

Over the last few decades, we've come to learn that optimal learning does not take place in a punitive environment. Teachers are taught to have *patience* when teaching, and this patience is enhanced by teachers being taught to have an understanding of why children fail to learn quickly, why they might resist learning, and why they might fail to act as requested. The concept of non-punitive instruction has, by now, reached a point where it's considered common knowledge that punishment is no longer seen as an effective or viable 'teaching tool' within *any* learning environment.

In addition, science has also discovered that the brain cognitively processes the learning of expected behaviors in the same way it processes other cognitive learning, such as learning how to read. Nevertheless, we continue to teach behavior through punishment largely unabated. Truth is, we should no more punish children for making repeated mistakes in learning how to read than punish them for repeated mistakes in learning how to behave. Likewise, we shouldn't attempt to force a child to learn how to read, anymore than we should attempt to force a child to learn acceptable behaviors. Both approaches are fraught with risk and can even prove to be counter-productive.

There may be a number of reasons as to why we may have continued to more closely associate 'discipline' with 'punishment' more so than associating 'discipline' with 'teaching'. Some of the reasons for this might include: 1. Our deeply ingrained orientation toward punishment developed during our formative years; 2. A related propensity for retribution; 3. The traditional concept of forcing children to respect authority (or authoritarian adults).

I'm sure we can all appreciate having observed that when it comes to 'getting even' against those who have offended our sensibilities, small children make easy targets. Related to this, we also know that many parents are very quick to feel offended when it comes to the issue of children failing to display acceptable levels of respect. And, at times, these parents can be found demanding their due respect through force. Another related factor that serves to compound this 'respect issue' involves our socially traditional propensity to confuse 'respect' with 'fear'... fact is, we can certainly teach fear through coercion, but we cannot teach respect in that same manner. But, as things stand, we still generally tend to equate respect with fear or awe, instead of the actual definition that describes 'respect' as holding another or others in high regard/high esteem.

I would say that Positive Discipline is more a matter of *attitude* toward children. It's an approach toward child rearing that is: 1. Dependent on an understanding of why children behave as they do; 2. A tolerance toward their developmental inabilities; 3. An added patience that comes with an increased awareness of their behavior.

One might ask for an example of Positive Discipline. Well, in answering that question, I'd recommend that when a child makes a mistake, a parent should go right on attempting to effectively *teach*. Some form of punishment would only halt, defeat, or possibly counter the educational process and the goal of the lesson. As I've said, coercion does not a good teacher make.

OUTCOMES OF POSITIVE DISCIPLINE

There's certainly a great deal of concern about what might happen to kids who are not spanked or otherwise punished. And because most people are familiar with the more severe consequences of spanking, such as physical and/or emotional harm being caused, I'd like to discuss a best-case scenario where children are raised in a totally non-punitive environment. An environment where children are taught *all* things without being forced, struck, humiliated, berated, or otherwise treated in a disrespectful manner.

I'm qualified to present this scenario with confidence as my own children were raised in such a manner. What are the long term outcomes of Positive Discipline? Let me illustrate by describing my adult son and daughter.

1. They both say that they are relatively happy, stress-free individuals compared to most.

2. They are both altruistic, and have been so from an exceptionally early age.

3. They are warm, caring, tolerant, confident in themselves, and authentic, which has left them with an extraordinary number of loving friends.

4. They have both been described by various people throughout the years as 'centered', 'grounded', 'self-actualized', 'highly emotionally sophisticated', 'beautiful human beings', and 'possessed of a high level of emotional maturity'.

I believe it is the high level of their self-esteem that serves as armor against stress, and on occasions when they do feel stressed, they are extremely resilient and quick to recover.

MY EXPERIENCE WITH POSITIVE DISCIPLINE

The qualifications and credentials related to my professional background pale drastically in comparison to the significance of my parenting experiences. I've had the great privilege to have raised two children
who eventually went on to become adults of exceptional inner-beauty
and strength. Who they have become as human beings has acted to
firmly cement my attitudes and beliefs toward child rearing approaches,
child behavior, and learning theory. As a result, most of what I once
held as theory, possibility, speculation, and hope related to child rearing practices, has since taken the form of confirmed proof in my eyes.
That which I once expressed with wary caution has evolved into a
strong sense of conviction. It's a conviction that came to pass over the
years through the seemingly 'magical' wonder I've so enjoyed witness-
ing in the growth and development of my kids throughout their lives. In
addition, there is the benefit of the surprising ease of parenting that
results from the simple existence of mutual adoration and respect.

There later came a time when I found myself faced with the realization that my kids had reached a level of emotional sophistication and
maturity that left me looking like a knuckle-dragging cave-dweller in
comparison (although this never diminished my feeling a sense of great
fulfillment and gratification). I must say that while it can be a humbling
experience to see your children reach a level of personal growth which
exceeds your own, it is nevertheless an experience of such profound
magnitude that one is filled with a sense of knowing what it is to live life
to its fullest. It is such an enriching, affirming, gratifying realization to
experience that I dearly wish every parent of every child could one day
come to know it.

I was a cheerleader for my kids. They've informed me of a number
of related childhood memories, and neither can recall any negative
memories or lingering negative consequences of being praised or rewarded. Of possibly related significance, as children they always felt
that I was 'on their side', and could be counted-on to 'be there' for them
regardless of the circumstances.

From my standpoint, they were adored from the get-go, and I would
submit that this adoration provided them with a sense of worth, and
unquestioned security. In turn, the satisfaction of these basic needs for
love and acceptance allowed them to developmentally move on to seek

the satisfaction of higher needs at an accelerated pace during their formative years. And, as a directly related consequence of this process, they developed a high level of self-esteem, independence, confidence, and emotional strength.

My kids were given extrinsic rewards for helping me with work or chores that served my own self-interests, but failed to serve theirs. The exception to this came when they would pitch in and help out just to be with me. Later, they simply chose to exercise their developing sense of teamwork and group cooperation by volunteering to 'help the cause'. They were also rewarded with my praise... heartfelt, sincere praise that served to convey my approval of them as people. It was always nurturing, reaffirming praise that also conveyed the depth of my love, gladness for their gladness, and a pride in who they were. It was praise that provided them with a sense of empowerment and importance in this world. Teamwork develops when children are not forced into work that fails to serve their self-interests. Responsibility is not taught, it's a developmental process.

I thought they were wonderful, lovely people and I told them so... what a disservice it would have been to not share such feelings with them. And, because they could always count on my sincerity, and knew that I honored them as human beings who were worthy of dignity and respect, they tended to respect and consider what I told them. If I had ever unwittingly praised them in way that left them feeling un-nurtured, uncomfortable, or even manipulated, they must have been very quick to forgive my mistake. And why not?

Shouldn't kids experience the knowledge that their parents love them more than anyone, and think more highly of them than the other adults they encounter in the world around them? Is it so hard to fathom that a child might come to feel that 'mommy can be forgiven for too much gushing over me once in a while because she loves me so much'? According to some, my praises should have caused the kids to become 'conditioned' into needy 'praise seekers'. Fact is, they were anything but. On the contrary, they had come to *know* that they were good, competent, and worthwhile young people.

This positive self-concept provided them with a sufficiently high level of independence and strength to enable them to develop a desire to function as their own agents from very early on. They were quick to stand up for themselves, and have always been leaders among their peers and numerous close friends. The people in their lives are more likely to come to *them* for praise, affirmation, approval, or support, rather than the other way around. Their strength (self-esteem) leaves them with little need to display more typically seen needs to reaffirm acceptability, gain reassurance, or be dependent upon the approval of others in an attempt to quell insecurities.

A VIEW OF CHILDREN

When I catch the eye of a young child, I feel a little lighter and a smile pulls at the corners of my mouth, regardless of how my day is going. There seems to be something wondrously human about this. Maybe it's because I'm looking into little searching eyes that say, 'Hi, you're an interesting fellow, do you like me?' Or, perhaps it's because what I see in those eyes is a beauty yet unmarred by life's slings and arrows, those sufferings that might later leave those eyes hiding behind a mask of cautious pretense. But, before such a time, what I see is a pure, open honesty that seems to ask for nothing more than gentle regard and a sharing of warmth. I can also see a vivacious, boundless zest for life that asks, 'What can we do now? What can I learn next? Let's live life to the hilt! What in the world is that? Let's go for it! Why is that? Let's laugh and play until we drop! Let's do it all at once! Could you give me a hug in the meantime?'

And, as that young child goes along their way, I feel a boost in my spirits at having looked into the eyes of the purist beauty humanity has to offer. It's often on these occasions that I'm reminded of raising my own children, and I remember attempting to raise them in a way that said, 'It would be my honor to teach you the ways of life, for you belong to the world just as it belongs to you. And, my little ones, it is my distinct pleasure to have been blessed with the good fortune to be the caretaker of your beauty and goodness until your dreams spread beyond the reach of my protective embrace'.

It seems to me that we should respect and honor this beauty of our young like nothing else in the world. We can respect their beauty by treating them as we would wish to be treated; we can honor them by learning all that we can about what makes for such beauty; and we can insure the continuance of their purity of love and goodness by teaching them those difficult lessons we expect them to learn by regarding them with the gentle, patient hand of loving guidance as best we can. It certainly worked for me as my beautiful children grew into beautiful adults.

Concluding Remarks

I realize that I haven't made many positive references to the state of child rearing in the U.S. or of our societal views toward children. Many believe that parenting is a burdensome chore, yet choose to have children regardless. Well, based on my parenting experience, I would like to strongly suggest that parenting can be a joyful experience. Why not make it yours?

There are no fancy tricks involved. My kids were born beautiful and simply remained that way. They never experienced the 'terrible two's' or the 'rebellious teenage years' because there was no need for these so-called 'stages' to occur. Some have found my claim hard to accept, but it's actually a sound, basic principle... love, adoration, and respect toward children is highly prone to be returned in equal measure. The end result tends to manifest itself in mutual trust, cooperation, and caring. For parents who understand the concept of Positive Discipline, child rearing becomes a simple matter of gentle, patient teaching.

I'm well aware of the fact that the road to Positive Discipline is not open to those who refuse change. After twelve years of posting on parenting boards, I've come to realize that a good number of parents remain stuck in the child rearing practices of their own parents. But, I have reached a number of those parents who have come to realize that their own harsh upbringings would be unacceptable for *their* children. Hopefully, this book will reach even more of those parents.

It's hard to imagine anyone arguing against the notion that what is needed most in this world is an increased level of altruistic behavior. What it is that I've offered in this book is a way in which we can most successfully accomplish that goal.

And, I must once again thank my philosophical mentor, A.S. Neill. It was his work that served as the inspirational guide on the long road I have traveled. Unlike him, I'm not a visionary. I simply learned and evolved.

Online References And Resources

Positive Discipline Resources

A. S. Neill's Summerhill School
http://www.summerhillschool.co.uk/

Positive Parenting
http://www.positiveparenting.com/resources/resources.html

Positive Parenting Message Board
http://messageboards.ivillage.com/iv-pppponline

Twenty Alternatives to Punishment by Aletha Solter, Ph.D.
http://www.awareparenting.com/twenty.htm

Parenting Without Punishing
http://www.nopunish.net/

Spanking Related Issues

Slapping and Spanking in Childhood and Its Association with Lifetime
Prevalence of Psychiatric Disorders
http://www.cmaj.ca/cgi/gca?sendit=Get+All+Checked+Abstract%28s%29&SEA
RCHID=1041949468944_779&TITLEABSTRACT=Slapping+and+spanking+in+
Childhood&JOURNALCODE=&FIRSTINDEX=0&hits=1&RESULTFORMAT=&g
ca=161%2F7%2F805

Research on Corporal Punishment – Available Online
http://stoptherod.net/research.htm

Corporal Punishment - Empirical Studies
http://pubpages.unh.edu/~mas2/CP-Empirical.htm

The Research and Informed Expert Opinion
http://nospank.net./resrch.htm

Slapping and Spanking in Childhood and Its Association With Lifetime
Prevalence of Psychiatric Disorders in a General Population
http://www.cmaj.ca/cgi/content/full/161/7/805

States Should Ban Violence Against Children – United Nations Study
http://nospank.net/n-q33r.htm

Correlation Between High Rates of Corporal Punishment in Public Schools and Social Pathologies
http://nospank.net./correlationstudy.htm

Experts - Spanking Harms Children, Especially Girls
http://nospank.net./women.htm

Spanking and Mental Illness
http://nospank.net./falk2.htm

The Sexual Dangers of Spanking Children
http://parentinginjesusfootsteps.org/sxdangers.html

Spanking Can Be Sexual Abuse
http://www.nospank.net/101.htm

Spanking, Pain and Pleasure
http://www.nospank.net/r-ali.htm

American Academy of Pediatrics' Position on Physical Punishment
http://nospank.net./aap4-c.htm

ChildAdvocate.org - Corporal Punishment Society's Acceptable Violence Towards Children
http://www.childadvocate.org/1a_research.htm

What Does Research Say About the Effects of Physical Punishment on Children?
http://www.extension.umn.edu/distribution/familydevelopment/components/7266a.html

The Neurobiology of Child Abuse
http://www.nospank.net/teicher2.htm

It's Time to Change 'The American Way of Discipline' - Arthur Cherry, M.D., FAAP,
http://nospank.net./aap5-a.htm

Why Do We Need Full Legal Reform to End All Corporal Punishment?
http://nospank.net./endallcp.htm

Physical Punishment of Children
http://nospank.net./shrc.htm

Corporal Punishment in Schools
http://aappolicy.aappublications.org/cgi/content/full/pediatrics%3b106/2/343

Lowest Achieving Ohio Schools Quickest With The Paddle-Rights
http://nospank.net./ohio3.htm

Dr. Spock on Parenting (1989)--Excerpts
http://nospank.net./spock2.htm

The Center for Effective Discipline, Columbus, Ohio
http://www.stophitting.com/

End All Corporal Punishment of Children
http://www.neverhitachild.org/

Corporal Punishment and Trauma - Building Better Health
http://healthresources.caremark.com/topic/corporal

Corporal Punishment of Children (Spanking)
http://www.religioustolerance.org/spanking.htm

Giving Guidance on Child Discipline
http://www.bmj.com/cgi/content/full/320/7230/261

The Belt, Adrenalin, and Delinquency
http://www.nospank.net/welsh5.htm

Abused Tots Take On Abusive Parents Ways
http://www.nospank.net/tots.htm

Impact of Parenting Styles - Alfred Adler Institute of San Francisco
http://ourworld.compuserve.com/homepages/hstein/parentin.htm

Adult Consequences of Childhood Parenting Styles - Alfred Adler Institute
http://ourworld.compuserve.com/homepages/hstein/adult.htm

Ten Reasons Not to Hit Your Kids - The Natural Child Project
http://www.naturalchild.com/jan_hunt/tenreasons.html

Guidance for Effective Discipline
http://aappolicy.aappublications.org/cgi/content/full/pediatrics%3b101/4/723

Spanking Strikes Out
http://life.familyeducation.com/spanking/discipline/36133.html

Corporal Punishment
http://www.infidels.org/library/historical/robert_ingersoll/corporal_punishment.html

Force and Fear Have No Place in Education
http://nospank.net/einstein.htm

Physical Punishment and The Development of Aggressive and Violent
Behavior - A Review, by Elizabeth Kandel
http://www.neverhitachild.org/areview.html

Let's Outlaw Any Hitting of Children
http://www.nospank.net/lndsbrg3.htm

Hitting People Is Wrong - and Children Are People Too
http://www.neverhitachild.org/hitting1.html

The Institute for the Study of Anti-Social Behaviour in Youth - Highlights from
the Latest Youth Update
http://www.iay.org/youth_update/abstracts_latest_issue.html#Maltreatment%20
and%20its%20Impact%20on%20C

Why Do We Hurt Our Children - The Natural Child Project
http://www.naturalchild.com/james_kimmel/punishment.html

Alternatives to Spanking
http://life.familyeducation.com/spanking/discipline/36135.html

Some Thoughts On Spanking - The Natural Child Project
http://www.naturalchild.com/guest/don_fisher.html

Raising Kind Children
http://extension.missouri.edu/xplor/hesguide/humanrel/gh6126.htm

Why You Should Say 'No' to Corporal Punishment - It Doesn't Work
http://archive.southcoasttoday.com/daily/05-96/05-27-96/c02li081.htm

Spanking - An Idea Whose Time Has Gone
http://nospank.net/gurza.htm

Faut-il interdire la fessée? / Should Spanking Be Prohibited?
http://www.nospank.net/n-j48.htm

The Swedish Example
http://parentinginjesusfootsteps.org/crowell-article.html

German Parliament Bans Use Of Corporal Punishment In
Child Rearing
http://nospank.net/deut.htm

Denmark Bans Spanking
http://www.neverhitachild.org/denmark1.html

Israeli High Court on Spanking
http://nospank.net/n-g02.htm

Jerusalem Supreme Court: Corporal Punishment of Children
Is Indefensible
http://nospank.net/israel.htm

Greece Outlaws Corporal Punishment in the Home
http://nospank.net/greece.htm

South Africa's Constitutional Court Says 'NO' to Spankers in
Christian Schools
http://nospank.net/sacourt2.htm

Spanking of Toddlers to Be a Crime in Scotland
http://www.nospank.net/n-i48.htm

Bangladesh Observes Child Rights Week
http://www.nospank.net/n-f33.htm

BBC News - UK - Smacking Children 'Does Not Work'
http://news.bbc.co.uk/2/hi/uk_news/252607.stm

Delhi School Kids To Be Spared The Rod
http://nospank.net/delhi.htm

Punjab Bans Corporal Punishment
http://nospank.net/pkstn.htm

No Smacking Rule For Children Under Three
http://www.scotland.gov.uk/News/Releases/2001/09/161

Greece outlaws corporal punishment in the home
http://nospank.net/greece.htm

End All Corporal Punishment of Children
http://www.endcorporalpunishment.org/

Correlation Between Corporal Punishment and Social Pathologies
http://nospank.net/guthrow.htm

Paddling States v. Non-Paddling States: A National Academic Comparison
http://nospank.net/charles5.htm

National Society for the Prevention of Cruelty to Children Call For Government
Rethink On Hitting Children Following United Nations Report
http://nospank.net/n-j58.htm

Corporal Punishment of Children (Spanking): Introduction and Legality
http://www.religioustolerance.org/spankin2.htm

Kenyan Children Suffer Frequent Beatings by Teachers
http://hrw.org/english/docs/1999/09/09/kenya1654.htm

Dept of Health Issues Guidelines to British Parents on How to Smack Their Children
http://wsws.org/articles/2000/feb2000/smck-f02.shtml

Project NoSpank
http://nospank.net./main.htm

Spanking Articles at findarticles.com
http://findarticles.com/

End All Corporal Punishment of Children - States With Full Abolition
http://endcorporalpunishment.org/pages/frame.html

The Center for Effective Discipline
http://www.stophitting.com/

Parenting Tips
http://familydoctor.org/online/famdocen/home/children/parents/behavior/368.html

Spanking - Ages 6 to 12 | ahealthyme.com
http://www.ahealthyme.com/topic/spanking6to12

Family Resource Library Resources
http://pubpages.unh.edu/~mas2/

A Good Whuppin'? Many Who Survived Childhood Spankings Now Endorse Them, Renewing Debate Over a Peculiar Institution.
http://www.childprotectionreform.org/policy/spanking/washpoststory.htm

Our Children Don't Deserve to Be Beaten
http://nospank.net/lombardo.htm

Monadnock Area Psychotherapy and Spirituality Services
http://www.mapsnh.org/spanking.html

Family Issue Facts, Spanking, Bulletin 4357
http://www.umext.maine.edu/onlinepubs/htmpubs/4357.htm

United Nations Committee on Rights of Child
http://www.nospank.net/uncrc.htm

Corporal Punishment Society's Acceptable Violence Towards Children
http://www.childadvocate.org/1a_research.htm

How Children Really React to Control
http://nospank.net/gordon.htm

Force and Fear Have No Place in Education
http://nospank.net/einstein.htm

Selected Print Medial Coverage
http://www.nospank.net/clips.htm

Let's Outlaw Any Hitting of Children
http://www.nospank.net/lndsbrg3.htm

Domestic Abuse Organizational and Employee Impact
http://www.newfoundations.com/OrgTheory/Mickles721.html

Plain Talk About Spanking
http://nospank.net/pt2007.htm

Brain Development:
The Effects of Abuse and Neglect

The Developing Brain and Child Abuse
http://www.ceunit.com/TheDevelopingBrainandChildAbuse_continuing
education

Causes and Mechanisms of Linear Growth Retardation
http://www.unu.edu/unupress/food2/UID06E/uid06e0t.htm

Late Outcome Following Central Nervous System Injury in Child Abuse
http://www.springerlink.com/content/dcrfynw07yuw5a3c/

Child Abuse Can Cause Permanent Damage to the Brain, Body, and Emotional
Well-Being
http://multipleminds.blogspot.com/2005/04/child-abuse-can-cause-permanent-
damage.html

The Effect of Childhood Trauma on Brain Development
http://www.leadershipcouncil.org/1/res/brain.html

Crime and Punishment

Juvenile Justice Bulletin -- June 2000 -- Research Studies and Results
http://www.ncjrs.gov/html/ojjdp/2000_6_3/page4.html

 Adult Hysteria Ignores the Facts
http://www.cjcj.org/pubs/index.php

CNN - Justice Department Study Says Juvenile Killings Decreased – 9/18/99
http://www.cnn.com/US/9909/18/crime.youth/index.html

Runaway Juvenile Crime- The Context of Juvenile Arrests in America
http://www.cjcj.org/pubs/runaway/runaway.html

Juvenile Justice Issues
http://www.buildingblocksforyouth.org/issues/

Young Criminals Not Just Sign of the Times
http://www.post-gazette.com/regionstate/19981025kids2.asp

The Influence of Corporal Punishment on Crime - The Natural Child Project
http://www.naturalchild.com/research/corporal_punishment.html

Office of Juvenile Justice and Delinquency Prevention -
Statistical Briefing
http://ojjdp.ncjrs.org/ojstatbb/

Bureau of Justice Statistics
http://www.ojp.usdoj.gov/bjs/cvict_c.htm

Spanking For God

A Critique of Growing Kids God's Way
http://www.rapidnet.com/~jbeard/bdm/exposes/ezzo/ezzokids.htm

Salon Mothers Who Think - Getting wise to 'Babywise'
http://www.salon.com/mwt/feature/1998/08/cov_06feature.html

Boot Camp for Babies
http://www.fix.net/~rprewett/bootcamp.html

James Dobson - Focusing on Himself - By Brian McKinley
http://elroy.net/ehr/dobson.html

James Dobson - Leader of the 'Focus on the Family' Cult
http://www.skeptictank.org/hs/dobson.htm

James Dobson's Gospel
http://www.psychoheresy-aware.org/dobson66.html

Christianity Today Magazine – Special News Report- Unprepared to Teach
http://www.ctlibrary.com/ct/2000/november13/6.70.html

The Fear of Being Permissive - The Natural Child Project
http://www.naturalchild.org/sidney_craig/permissive.html

Lawyer Wants Light Sentence For Beatings With Heavy Stick
http://nospank.net/n-j68.htm

World Corporal Punishment Research - Church Renews
Spanking Debate, 4/2001
http://www.corpun.com/usd00104.htm

Related Topics

CNN - Surgeon General Issues Call to Action to Prevent Suicides - July 28, 1999
http://www.cnn.com/HEALTH/9907/28/suicide.prevention/index.html

CNN - New Study Finds No Harm to Children of Working Moms – 2/28/99
http://www.cnn.com/US/9902/28/working.moms/

1996 Human Rights Report - Sweden
http://www.state.gov/www/global/human_rights/1996_hrp_report/sweden.html

Ontario Consultants on Religious Tolerance - Slavery From Biblical Times Until
Now
http://www.religioustolerance.org/slavery.htm

Harvard Researchers Say Children Need Touching and Attention - The Natural
Child Project
http://www.naturalchild.com/research/harvard_attention.html

The Sleep Well
http://www.stanford.edu/~dement/children.html

CNN - Environment Tops Kids' List of Concerns - December 13, 1999
http://archives.cnn.com/1999/nature/12/13/kids.environment.enn/index.html

BabyCenter - The Ferber Method Demystified
http://www.babycenter.com/refcap/7755.html

Journal Article about ADHD, ADD, Ritalin Hazards by Peter R. Breggin, MD
and Ginger Ross Breggin
http://www.breggin.com/methylphen.html

Topic - Ritalin
http://www.eagleforum.org/topics/ritalin/ritalin.html

Reactive Attachment Disorder – It's Time To Understand
http://members.tripod.com/~radclass/

Thoughts on Punishment - The Natural Child Project
http://www.naturalchild.com/sidney_craig/punishment.html

Just the Facts About Sexual Orientation & Youth - A Primer
for Principals, Educators and School Administrations
http://www.apa.org/pi/lgbc/publications/justthefacts.html

Fifty Years of Research and the Big Controversy
http://adsg.syix.com/

Who's in Control - by Jean Liedloff
http://www.continuum-concept.org/reading/whosInControl.html

The Baumrind Fallacy
http://nospank.net./baumrind.htm

Parents Beware - Youth Training Camps and Programs
http://nospank.net./beware.htm

107 Organizations Call For An End To Corporal Punishment In
U.S. Schools
http://nospank.net./endcp.htm

Personality, Temperament, Psychopathology, & Emotion Tests
& Software
http://www.kaaj.com//psych/scales/

Alice Miller - The Childhood Trauma
http://www.vachss.com/guest_dispatches/alice_miller2.html

Charges Filed Against Boot Camp Leaders
http://www.nospank.net/n-i88.htm

Deep Are the Roots
http://www.nospank.net/hitler.htm

Facts About Homosexuality and Child Molestation
http://psychology.ucdavis.edu/rainbow/html/facts_molestation.html

The Sudbury Valley School.
http://www.sudval.org/

Siegel, "'The Rule of Love'...," 1996
http://womhist.binghamton.edu/vawa/prologue.htm

Would You Trust This Man Alone With Your Dog?
http://nospank.net/dugan.htm